HAUNTED
BATH

HAUNTED
BATH

DAVID BRANDON

The
History
Press

First published 2009
Reprinted, 2019

The History Press
97 St George's Place, Cheltenham,
Gloucestershirem GL50 3QB
www.thehistorypress.co.uk

British Library Cataloguing in Publication Data.
A catalogue record for this book is available from the British Library.

ISBN 978 0 7524 4759 9

Typesetting and origination by The History Press
Printed in Great Britain by TJ International Ltd, Padstow, Cornwall.

CONTENTS

One   A Selective and Irreverent Outline History of Bath   7

Two   Ghosts and Other Spooky Spectres   19

Three   Central Bath   23

Four   Around Bath   83

ONE

A SELECTIVE AND IRREVERENT OUTLINE HISTORY OF BATH

Bath has always been a special place. It is a place where riches, fashion and style have frequently stood in stark contrast next to hypochondria, dissipation, raffishness, poverty and crime. Here we trace aspects of Bath's history to provide a background to the odd and often spooky stories in the main section.

The hot mineral springs of Bath attracted interest before the Romans arrived; the pre-Roman Britons had had a goddess called Sul, whose name was incorporated into the later Roman name for Bath - which was *Aquae Sulis*. The legend of how the beneficial effects of this water were discovered is a strange one and worth repeating.

It is said that the founder of Bath was Bladud, the son of Hudibras, King of ancient Britain. He was a virtuous young man who contracted leprosy and had to leave his father's court for fear of passing the condition on to others. His mother, distraught at the involuntary banishment of her son but hoping that he might find a cure, gave him a distinctive ring to wear on his finger so that he might be able to make himself known if and when he returned.

Bladud wandered around disconsolately and, needing to make a living, became a swineherd. To his dismay he realised that he had passed on his leprosy to the pigs. One day he noticed how eagerly they plunged into some boggy marshland nearby. He had some difficulty persuading them to come out, using acorns as a bribe. When the mud had dried off, to his amazement he saw that the leprosy had gone. Without further ado, Bladud himself leapt into the quagmire and emerged without any trace of the dreaded leprosy. He rushed to his father's court, flashing the ring as he went in, to be greeted rapturously by all concerned. Bladud was so grateful to the curative waters, or shall we say mud, that he hastened back and founded a settlement which was the origin of the beautiful city of Bath.

It is evident is that the Romans appreciated the warm, saline and health-giving waters which bubbled to the surface at Bath. They probably colonized Bath early during their occupation and even then the city took on something of the character which it was to display to the full in Georgian days – as both a resort for those with health problems and a place of recreation and relaxation, often of a somewhat debauched nature. The irony is that the overindulgence in sensual pleasures which has always been a feature of Bath's activities was likely to undo whatever good the therapy was intended to promote.

Bladud's Head

England was only a minor outpost of their far-flung empire and the Romans didn't think much of it except that it provided grain and some useful minerals. Bath became a small provincial town containing a health resort centred on the baths, the presence of which would have brought some prosperity to the locality. The Romans were highly impressed by the waters which gushed up hot and bubbling from an unfathomable depth to the tune of half a million gallons a day. They bathed in the waters and gulped them down greedily, convinced that their health was benefiting as they did so. Masseurs, physicians, and quacks plied their trade around the baths. Also attracted was a sub-class of tavern-keepers, musicians, confidence-tricksters, pimps and procurers who would undoubtedly have been able to cater for every known vice. Many of the Romans who came to Bath were of what we would now call senior and middle management status and were accompanied by coveys of young boys who pandered to all their mentors' needs.

Some who came were seeking relief from such afflictions as gout and the rheumatics which the miserable English climate made worse. Other Romans came because they identified Sul with Minerva, the goddess of healing, and they made the town into a shrine or temple to her. A number of altars exist which are evidence of this. These glory days of Bath ended somewhere around AD 400 when Britain descended into what is so misleadingly termed the Dark Ages.

What put Bath back on the map as it were was the founding of a major Benedictine abbey in the tenth century. Such establishments provided employment and encouraged the development of retailing and service industries. There is some evidence that the Normans started using the baths again because the King's Bath is named after Henry I. For three or more centuries, the abbey administered the baths and derived income from doing so.

The abbey also maintained a hospice for poor people who came to Bath seeking cures. As with so many other settlements where there was a major monastic establishment, relations between town and gown were not always particularly friendly. There were constant disputes over property matters, but a choice one concerned the ringing of the bells in 1408. The abbey claimed the right to ring the bells first and last with the city's various parish churches having to fit in between as best they could and only when they had received a pre-arranged signal from the abbey. The mayor, the townsfolk and parishioners objected to the high-handed way in which this was done and so they decided, all of them, to ring their bells for twenty-four hours without stopping. This was very silly. It created a terrible din and generated much acrimony which rumbled on until 1421 when the King stepped in and decided in favour of the abbey.

From the early thirteenth century there had been a mayor and corporation of Bath and the city enjoyed extensive privileges granted by the Crown and the abbey. We know that there were five medieval parish churches in Bath, all of which have been destroyed or changed beyond recognition. Bath was clustered around the abbey and circumscribed by the hills with which it is surrounded and visitors in the fifteenth century commented that it had scarcely spread beyond its walls with their four gates.

It is likely that local sufferers from a range of conditions, including leprosy, made use of the waters. Some were attracted to the baths for reasons other than therapy, and gave the place a bad reputation. In 1449 the Bishop of Bath and Wells was forced to speak out about the unashamed nude mixed bathing that was taking place. So depraved were some of the bathers that whenever a genuine seeker after the cure tried to enter the water wearing a costume, he or she would be seized, manhandled and stripped, the whole process being accompanied by a barrage of catcalls and jeers from the onlookers

To the visitor in the 1500s, Bath would have given first and foremost the impression of an episcopal and monastic city. One outstanding work was the start of the rebuilding of the decrepit abbey. The days of Bath as a seat of monasticism were, however, numbered. In the summer of 1535, Dr Richard Layton, one of the most unpleasant of Thomas Cromwell's commissioners, visited Bath to assess the wealth of the abbey. His estimate of its financial potential made it clear that it was ripe for the picking but he seemed more interested in the goings-on within Bath's monastic community. His report dwelt with prurient relish on the buggery and adultery his investigations had unearthed and claimed that some of the brethren had ten women who they 'enjoyed' while others, less fortunate, had to make do with only eight. The abbey was dissolved – it probably deserved it – but worse followed when the citizens systematically stripped it of all its glass, ironwork, lead and its bells which they sold off to the highest bidders. All that was left of the abbey was a shell, some of which no longer had a roof. Money was eventually found to restore the building but this work was not completed until the reign of James I, which started in 1603.

What of the baths in the sixteenth century? Dr William Turner, Dean of Wells, wrote a treatise on the baths of England, Germany and Italy and made it clear that the rich and fashionable had little time for Bath and preferred to visit overseas health resorts. However he produced a list of do's and don'ts for those using the medicinal waters. He recommended that the waters should only be taken after purging one's sins by confession but also, and he was very insistent on this, after purging the bowels. The true seeker after a cure, Turner said, should keep himself chaste from women for at least one month after taking the waters. In 1572 another book on bathing appeared, in this case written by a Dr Jones. His guidance was similar to that of Dr Turner but he added that for complaints below the stomach, the bather should place himself in water up to the navel and for problems above the navel, he should immerse himself right up to the neck. Dr Jones was insistent on a strict segregation of the sexes, warning his readers, who were assumed to be men, to avoid copulation at all costs, adding tactfully for those who had not realised it, that copulation was 'the use of women'.

However in 1616 Anne of Denmark, the wife of King James I, visited Bath for its healing springs and from that day, things began to look up. Nothing attracted fashionable attention like a royal endorsement and no sooner had the Queen got there than the rich and fashionable started to flock to the city. The facilities were, however, pretty grim. As one observer tartly commented, 'The baths were like so many bear gardens and modesty was entirely shut out of them; people of both sexes bathing by day and night naked and with dogs and cats in large numbers'. The baths were open to the air and all manner of filth landed in them including leaves, litter and dead birds. Their users thought nothing of urinating or defecating in them.

In the reign of Charles II, Bath became very fashionable as King and Court descended on it in 1663. Ostensibly they came to seek a cure for the Queen's apparent sterility. It is undoubtedly the Restoration that marked the real turning point in Bath's fortunes and saw the beginning of the extraordinary and unique role it was to play in the eighteenth century. The city's character began to change as more and more affluent people flocked there to see and be seen. The local manufacture and trading of wool and cloth declined as the place increasingly took on the character for which it was to become famous and which led to it becoming in effect the second city of England. While Bath was attracting the well-off seeking surcease from their ills, sometimes real but often imagined, the city was lacking in the kind of comforts and amenities needed to make their stay a congenial one. One visitor complained that apart from bathing there was little to do but to walk in the fields or play bowls. Bath was basically a small provincial town which just like all the others stank, had narrow, unpaved and filthy streets and clogged drains. It was largely unlit and dangerous, especially after dark.

Five men of exceptional qualities made eighteenth-century Bath what it became famous for. They were Beau Nash, Dr William Oliver, Ralph Allen and the two Woods, father and son. Of these, the Beau has probably enjoyed the most enduring fame. Let us see what he did for Bath.

Richard Nash, destined for fame as Beau Nash, arrived in Bath in the summer of 1702. He was twenty-eight years of age. His clothes were somewhat gaudy, he had a red, slightly fleshy face and he was a touch on the corpulent side. He was an inveterate gambler. He had very little money but was well aware that the city was becoming fashionable and was attracting the rich. From his experience, he knew that many such people were not over-endowed with brains.

He felt sure that he would be able to outwit them at the gaming tables and thereby end his financial embarrassment. In that sense he was a chancer. Bath was to prove to be full of chancers over the next 150 years.

So who was Richard Nash? He was born in 1674 in Swansea, the son of a sound but stolid businessman. Nash was educated at Carmarthen Grammar School and Jesus College, Oxford but he spent most of his time while he was there chasing the local girls and didn't get round to much studying. He went down without completing a degree, possibly sent down for his sexual activities, excessive even by Oxford undergraduate standards. He enlisted as a junior officer in the army but got bored and then studied law. He did not complete his studies. Nash clearly sowed his wild oats as a young man. He was only about seventeen when for a wager he had ridden through a village on a cow, stark naked and facing its tail. He was a little older when roistering with his companions he got so drunk that he passed out. When he woke up he was aboard a naval vessel into which he had been pressed. He served for several months during which time he sustained a serious leg injury in battle; the musket ball remaining embedded in his leg. At least that's what he told everybody.

In Bath, Nash discovered that he had two particularly valuable talents. He could organise and superintend social functions and he could command respect even from his social superiors. The city that Nash was visiting for the first time was attracting increasing numbers of visitors but it had little to offer them. In 1710 there were two small theatres and two coffee houses but no special room existed for water-drinking, the baths were still uncovered and there was no indoor place of assembly. There were gravel walks north-east of the abbey and close to the river where musicians performed every afternoon, but little hint of sophistication or elegance.

Within a short time, drawing on reserves of personality and fortitude that he probably did not know he possessed, Nash was the undisputed dictator and arbiter of the manners and mores of the city's elegant, polite society. He could quell a duchess with one withering look. This is all the more extraordinary given that he was merely of middling rank in society and neither physically large nor strikingly handsome. His trademark was a white, broad-brimmed beaver hat which he apparently carried with him at all times. When asked why he sported such a distinctive but unfashionable hat, he replied that it was because it was so distinctive that he could be sure it would never be stolen.

The problem with Bath at the time that Nash arrived was that no one had laid down the ground rules for the correct forms of behaviour in public. Those visitors who were of so-called noble birth looked down on other visitors who were from the gentry and they in turn took every opportunity to snub and humiliate those lower down the social ladder. Those who smoked did so in public with nobody to tell them that they shouldn't. People turned up improperly dressed at the balls. Card-players, many of whom were professional gamblers and some who were no more and no less than cheats, played the tables sometimes for twenty-four hours without a break. Scuffles in the street and duels were commonplace. Drunken brawls frequently took place especially between upper class young bloods and their favourite opponents, the sedan chairmen who were able to give a good account of themselves with the heavy wooden staves they used for carrying the chairs. The lodgings that were available were frequently dirty and pestiferous. Nash realised that Bath would soon find itself abandoned by the great and the good unless something was done.

Nash was highly intelligent. He recognised that there was money and status to be won by the person who could create some order and seemliness from the existing mess that was Bath and its facilities. Improvements were essential to widen the city's appeal and attract more people and more investment. He believed that he was the man to get the process going. When the existing Master of Ceremonies was killed in a duel, he took over.

The Beau immediately set to work. He drew up a set of rules for how to behave in Bath and to ignore these was to risk being ostracised or politely told to go elsewhere. In a very short time it became obvious that adhering to the rules actually made a stay at Bath a much more seemly affair.

However it was more difficult and expensive to deal with what we would now call the infrastructure of the city. Nash was extremely persuasive and convinced the right people that judicious investment would reap rich returns. If more of the right kind of people could be attracted to stay at Bath, the provision of the surroundings and services they needed would enrich the local business community. A rolling programme of improvements included effective cleaning, paving and lighting of the streets, upgrading of the baths, the provision of promenades and other social amenities and more and better accommodation. A proper pump room was completed in 1705 and a handsome Assembly Room was opened in 1708 where genteel entertainments were available on most nights of the week.

By sheer dint of his formidable personality and determination and the general perception that he was improving things in Bath, Nash went on to create more ground rules for which he brooked absolutely no deviance. He insisted that duelling and the wearing of swords be stopped, that women should cease to appear at prestigious social gatherings wearing white aprons and that men should not appear at them wearing riding boots. He banned smoking in Bath's public rooms just at a time when the popularity of pipe-smoking was at its height. Gossipers and scandalmongers were shunned. It took only a few seasons for Nash's writ to be accepted by virtually all residents and visitors to the town. There were tricky moments, however. The Duchess of Queensberry was a formidable and haughty beldame and she appeared at a glittering function wearing an apron. The conversation ceased and the chamber orchestra stopped sawing as Nash walked the length of the room, his jaw set and his brows beetling. He seized the apron, pulled it off and threw it to the Duchess's attendant ladies, observing in ringing tones as he did so that white aprons were only for 'abigails'. The Duchess took the point. Perhaps no one had ever stood up to her before. Nash had an acerbic wit. Someone, determined to pick an argument, suggested to Nash that he was immoral for having a mistress, to which Nash gave the immortal response, 'a man can no more be termed a whoremonger for having one whore in his house, than a cheesemonger for having one cheese'.

One of the activities of fashionable Bath which Nash kept his eye on but never managed completely to control was the activity of those searching for marriage and sex or, very frequently, just sex. There were more women in Bath during the season than men and many of these women were looking for matrimony for themselves or often for their daughters. Needless to say there were always plenty of men looking for sex and smaller numbers seeking matrimony. There were also many married women whose main concern was also to find sex. Their husbands might well be elsewhere and so they were eager for brief sexual adventures, no questions asked, no promises expected.

Bath attracted more than its fair share of rogues and those looking for easy pickings. After all, a fool and his money are soon parted. Nash did have a moral code of sorts and he made it his business to know who was in town and likely to be trying it on and who were likely to be the victims. He had a very effective intelligence network. He was undoubtedly responsible for saving a number of gullible young men from confidence tricksters and cardsharpers, and since he knew who the sexual predators were, he was able to whisper in the appropriate ear or even make the odd veiled threat, by doing so help to preserve some young lady's virtue, at least for the time being. Bath attracted charlatans and mountebanks like bees to honey. Most of them didn't get past Nash.

Nash was very good at wheedling money out of the rich but there is plenty of evidence that at least some of this he dispensed to various charities. He won widespread admiration from most of the wealthy patrons of Bath and dislike from only a few. It is known that he had the common touch and got on well with ordinary folk. Sometimes he even gave money from his winnings at the gaming table to those he considered needy, but deserving cases. He was, incidentally, never a particularly rich man. There were always rumours that he was a cheat at cards. It was also rumoured that he was a gigolo and he certainly seems to have been tipped by many well-to-do ladies of mature years for the provision of unspecified services.

As Beau Nash got older, his looks, which had never been particularly winsome, degenerated. His face took on a purplish hue, his eyes became watery and he grew several chins. He continued to cut something of a dash but no longer could he afford the coach in which he used to move around Bath, with its six dapple-grey horses, an outrider or two, footmen and a man blowing a French horn. He faded away from the Bath scene and died in relative obscurity and poverty.

In 1766 a quiet country parson called John Penrose took himself and his family to Bath for the first time. The reason ostensibly was to cure his gouty leg but he had a healthy curiosity to find out whether what he had heard about the place was true. We learn about what he saw from a series of lively letters he wrote to friends and relations. It is clear that he quickly took to the hustle and bustle. He was impressed by the company, pleased by the shops, amazed by the new buildings, amused by the vanity but also the splendour of the fashions on display, edified by a church service of solid dignity, gratified by seeing Prime Minister Pitt in the Pump-Room and felt that drinking the spa waters had a beneficial effect on his gout.

No other place in England outside London in the eighteenth and nineteenth centuries was so much written about as Bath, with the arguable exception of Brighton. Bath features in novels, in plays, in verse, in satire and, for its sins, it was rebuked in innumerable sermons. Antiquarians vied with each other to produce definitive histories of the place, painters and print-makers hurried to record its sights. Satirical cartoonists avidly encapsulated its many visible human follies. Bath's rise to eminence coincided with the coming of the Industrial Revolution, but while many other towns and cities became centres of manufacturing, trade or commerce, Bath was the pioneer in the development of a new service industry, that of leisure and hospitality.

It also became a centre for fashionable retailing, a role which it still manages to hang on to. It possessed many specialised shops, indicative of the considerable wealth of many of its visitors and a significant number of its residents. For this reason, florists prospered, as did retailers of snuff, perfumes, writing materials and fans. In 1755 we have a record of two ladies who established a shop dispensing breakfast, tea and newspapers close to the abbey, and a shop in Green Street which sold lawns, cambrics, velvet and lace. The Parade Coffee House supplied jellies at 4d a glass, whipped syllabubs and a range of mineral waters.

Bath was a beneficiary of the growth of the British economy on the eve of the Industrial Revolution. The outward signs of wealth – the increased consumption of food, expenditure on well-appointed houses, the preoccupation with fashion and the boom in books, music, entertainment and holidays – were all especially reflected in the rapid growth of leisure activities including those on offer at Bath. The rise of Bath was not simply down to the efforts of people like Nash. The times were right to bring out their talents. The city and a few other fashionable watering places had their heyday because of the growing prosperity of British agriculture and it was like the swan song of the old landed interest, the traditional ruling class of Britain, before the major growth of urban and industrial Britain and the emergence of a very different elite, the industrial and manufacturing bourgeoisie. Perhaps the old landed ruling class and its hangers-on were having their last fling, ostentatiously frittering away their time and money in a show of conspicuous consumption and, it could be said, conspicuous pointlessness. Their day was almost over. Georgian Bath, for all its beauty, represented the incipient decay of a class that had been overtaken by forces which it barely understood and certainly could not control.

Even during its peak years Bath had a dual character. Certainly it attracted many of Britain's most fashionable people and it offered them an unequalled range of expensive pastimes while they stayed in the city. Wherever the rich went, there was inevitably a sizeable gaggle of camp followers. Some were aristocratic rouees whose life was given over to dissipation and who lost fortunes at the gaming tables without turning a hair. Such people were often idle, vicious and volatile. Others were supremely stupid and gullible. Bath attracted parasitic and criminal elements, looking for quick and easy pickings. There were plenty to be had.

The pleasures of the flesh were available to those of both sexes who could pay, and sexual encounters took place in private lodgings or in brothels which often posed as lodging-houses and were found in substantial numbers in various parts of the city. Vicarious sexual pleasures were available in the pornographic literature of the period, of which much was available in bookshops in Bath. Typical of its genre was a book by Thomas Stretzer called *A New Description of Merryland* which, under the guise of being a serious study of topography, takes a trip around a woman's body with such features as 'Gardens of Delight'; Forests of Joy' and 'Mounds of Pleasure'. It was published in 1740 and such was its success that an illustrated version came out in 1741. The Bath bookseller who published it was a skilled publicist and he produced an anonymous pamphlet attacking 'Merryland' for being smutty and obscene. This of course guaranteed it even better sales.

The extent of prostitution and the concern felt about it is indicated by the founding of the Female Penitentiary and Lock Hospital in Walcot Street in 1805 as a place for rescuing fallen women and restoring them to useful employment. The women were regarded as sinners and ways had to be found for them to purge their sin. Nowadays we know that it was largely poor wages, unemployment, social conditions and simple ill-luck that drove women of the underclass into prostitution. Few such women were full-time prostitutes. They went out onto the streets when times were hard. Large numbers of the city's prostitutes were either in the sweated clothes-making trade or were domestic servants likely to be made jobless as soon as the Bath season was over. These women had short careers as prostitutes. What with poor diets, disease, alcohol abuse, hard physical work when they could get it and often large numbers of unplanned children, they were old by the time they were thirty. It is significant that prostitutes feature disproportionately as suicide victims in Bath and there were many who drowned themselves in the River Avon.

In 1597 a parliamentary act was passed which unintentionally made the phrase 'the Beggars of Bath' famous throughout the country. The act said that Bath's waters should be freely available to all those who needed them and in particular the 'diseased and impotent poor'. Parishes throughout England were encouraged to contribute towards the cost of sending their most needy cases to Bath. Beggars eagerly flocked to Bath and some of them may indeed have obtained relief from their ailments, but many others settled in the city which consequently gained a reputation for what we would now call 'antisocial behaviour'. Early in the eighteenth century the legislation was repealed but by this time the city was full of potentially rich pickings. It was not easy to get rid of the beggars. The council's writ only applied to the area within the medieval walls so the poor simply decamped over the river to the south and east of the city where there was nothing the council could do about them.

Consequently, such areas as Holloway and Widcombe became notorious for the behaviour of their inhabitants. The Dolemeads just to the east of the city were described as a 'perfect colony of vice and dissipation'. It was so low-lying that it was regularly flooded. No one lived there who could possibly afford to live elsewhere. For much of the eighteenth and nineteenth centuries the beggars headed into the city by day and returned to their 'extramural' hovels at night. In 1834 these areas were brought within the city's jurisdiction and they began to be properly policed.

A particularly notorious area was Kingsmead, centred on Avon Street, leading down to the river. Developed in the 1700s, it also was prone to regular flooding. At first it had been moderately fashionable but as the better-off moved out, so the thieves and prostitutes moved in and the area became a criminal rookery. It became the practice among the ultra-fashionable to go out in a large group and walk down Avon Street to gawp at the locals and think how pleasant it was not to have to live like the other half. When the area flooded, raw sewage coursed through the streets and waterborne diseases carved a swathe through the local population. In 1836, forty-nine people died during one cholera outbreak and twenty-seven of them lived in Avon Street.

The city was infested with the kind of low-life that preyed on innocent or inexperienced visitors. Much use was made of loaded dice while cardsharps would play with marked cards. Men known as 'rooks' hovered in the background of the gaming tables only too ready to lend money to those doing badly but feeling sure that their luck was just about to turn. Some would-be gamblers never got as far as the gaming tables. They would pop into a convivial tavern for a drink whereupon they would make the acquaintance of a friendly gentleman or two. They would get into conversation, the wine would flow and the artless victim would become drunk and insensible whereupon his pockets would be rifled or alternatively, he would be mugged in the street. One man ruined at the gambling tables hanged himself at the Bear Inn. A youth shot himself for the same reason, as did a wealthy lady of advanced years who should have known better than to stake everything on the roll of a dice. At least one detected cheat was thrown out of an upper-floor window while one had his hand pinned to the table with a fork. Many an argument ended in a duel.

A visit to Bath could sometimes be a risky business given the large number of highwaymen and footpads who hovered around the main roads leading into the city. Claverton Down, the main approach from the south, was particularly notorious and so riders and foot-travellers usually travelled in groups for mutual protection. An example of the kind of thing that could happen was when highwaymen stopped Dr Hancock in 1753 and fired a number of shots into his carriage which miraculously failed to hit anyone. They then seized his eight-year-old daughter and threatened to shoot her if he didn't hand over all his valuables immediately. One farmer from Batheaston had the dubious honour of being held up three times in two days.

One aspect of Bath that has not been mentioned yet concerns the elegant terraces, squares and crescents that draw the 'ums' and 'aahs' from the tourists on account of their apparently timelessly classical design. Behind the facades, these were not all they might appear. They were a bit like the proverbial basket of strawberries – what you could see were the good ones and what was behind could be pretty ropey. They may have looked good but they were often built as cheaply as possible and many corners were cut. There were of course no such things as building regulations in those days. Some builders built well. Others did not. In particular foundations were often inadequate and many houses settled within a short time of being built. You can see the result of this in parts of Pulteney Street, for example. Joists were used as sparingly as possible and floorboards frequently sank if a particularly heavy object was placed on them. A shortfall in the number of joists employed meant that front walls were sometimes insufficiently supported and they could move outwards. A survey in the 1930s of many of Bath's Georgian buildings raised the fear that if a bomb dropped at one end of Pulteney Street, the rest of the buildings would collapse like a pack of cards.

In many ways these must have been cheerless places in which to live. The high-ceilinged rooms were hard to heat and to keep warm. Skimping on the price of doors and other internal fittings meant awful draughts and bedrooms were so cold that most people slept behind the curtains of four poster beds. There was rarely any running water and servants had to carry coal, water and other necessities up and down innumerable flights of stairs. Their own quarters in the attics were notorious for being too cold in winter and too hot in summer. The lack of toilets was another aspect of life that wasn't so glamorous behind the glittering façade. Frequently pits were dug in the basement with boards over them containing a place for the backside. When these pits were nearly full, ashes or earth would be thrown in and another pit dug elsewhere close by. The stench, especially in the summer, must have been awful. Only the most well-to-do could afford for the night soil-men to come and empty their cesspits. If a Georgian lady announced that she was 'going to pluck a rose', this meant that she was going out into the garden to have a wee behind a shrub.

For almost two thousand years people have gone to Bath to take the waters, seeking a cure for a wide variety of ailments. Very early on it was claimed that Bath's waters would cure that scourge of medieval society, leprosy. Later it was believed that the waters could help relieve indigestion, referred to as 'worms in the belly', and gout. In addition the waters would ease limbs affected by rheumatism and the palsy, and it was claimed that they could cure sterility. Such a claim was bound to be a good money-spinner and as a result a succession of ladies, including some royals, came to Bath intent on trying to produce heirs. Even the authorities of course had to admit that the waters alone would not achieve conception. Not only sterility but problems like obesity, deafness and forgetfulness could be helped by a course of taking the waters, or so it was suggested.

Many people complained how unpleasant the baths were. The smell of sulphur and clouds of steam that met the bather were off-putting and caused profuse sweating and red, running eyes. Once bathing costumes came into use they tended to be stained brown by the water. Some bathers smoked tobacco while immersed in the water. Others of course did their number ones and number twos. Onlookers were always there in plenty and some openly scoffed at the more grotesque-looking of the bathers down below. Others hurled small coins at the bathers and these could hurt if they got the bather in the wrong place. Local hooligans were known to throw cats and dogs down on the bathers.

Even if these hazards are discounted, bathers suffering, for example, from festering open ulcers, sores and septic wounds, might be found wallowing in the water next to people with diseases of the internal organs who every so often would take a mouthful of the water intent on getting the

A ghostly old lady

full benefit of its therapeutic powers. Many of those enjoying a dip might well be taking their first bath for weeks or even months and would have been unspeakably dirty and smelly as they entered the water. No wonder that one cynical or perhaps realistic observer of the eighteenth century put it like this, 'it does one ten times more good to leave Bath than to go to it'.

If this was not enough, another observer, after describing the scene in the baths in rather uncomplimentary terms continues ,'…the spectators in the galleries please their roving fancies with this lady's face, another's breasts and a third's ample nates. In one corner stood an old lecher of at least three score years and ten, greedily and wishfully making love to a young lady nearby, she being no more than fourteen'.

This has been a highly selective but affectionate survey of Bath's recent history up to 1800. Now in the twenty-first century, Bath still cuts a dash. It is a favoured residential, retail and cultural centre which attracts British and overseas visitors in large numbers. Although the 1950s to the 1970s saw the loss of some fine buildings and the erection of others that are not just insensitive to their surroundings but are also architecturally illiterate, Bath is still a stunningly attractive city. Like many other cities in Britain, it has sharp contrasts between rich and poor and its share of deprivation and social exclusion. It manages to retain something of the raffishness of its past and is a place with considerable vitality. The author thinks Bath is a wonderful place.

TWO

GHOSTS AND OTHER SPOOKY SPECTRES

The ultimate mystery of life for most people is what happens to us when we die. Is the soul that makes each of us distinctive individuals simply snuffed out when the decay of our physical parts begins? It is hard to accept that the world with which we are so familiar continues after we have died and can apparently cope perfectly well without us. Is it not better to live in hope or belief that something survives after death; that there is an after-life? However, even this possibility is viewed by most of us with considerable trepidation.

Many of the world's religions are preoccupied with the issue of the continued existence of our souls after physical death. Indeed many religions teach that this life is merely a preparation for the next and that we will be judged by the Almighty when we die. If we receive a favourable appraisal when we die, the future is eternal happiness. The alternative is almost too awful to contemplate.

Most religions have created destinations for the souls of the departed. In the case of Christianity these are Heaven for the good and Hell, a state of permanent horror, for sinners. Some Christians believe in a kind of half-way house called Purgatory. Here the souls of those who are a particular mix of good and bad will be lodged temporarily while they are called to account and atone for their unredeemed misdemeanours. Sooner or later, they will either graduate to Heaven or descend into Hell.

If we believe that our souls live on in another world, it is only a small step to visualise the possibility of the dead returning to the living world under certain conditions. In many cultures, it has long been believed that the souls of the dead yearn to return to the scenes of their earthly lives and that they bitterly resent those that they knew who are still alive. The soul therefore might come back, seeking vengeance, particularly on someone who wronged it during its earthly life. Perhaps it wants to settle the hash of the person who murdered it.

On occasions the soul seems a trifle confused but seems to want to sort out things that were left unresolved or otherwise unsatisfactory when its owner died. Such matters might, for example, include the manner or place of the body's burial. On other occasions it may return to provide a warning to the living concerning their behaviour or perhaps an impending disaster. A prime time for the appearance of a soul is the anniversary of its death. Sometimes, perhaps, the soul appears to come back simply out of curiosity. Some seem intent on returning and continuing to perform the habitual actions they undertook when they were still alive. Yet others act as if they want to atone for the sins they committed. When it returns, the soul is said to be a ghost. These have fascinated and frightened mankind for thousands of years.

There are many ways in which ghostly phenomena manifest themselves. They may be seen or heard. Often though, people claiming to have had such experiences say that they have 'sensed' their activity or presence rather than having had a more tangible, easily described contact. Perhaps they have smelt the stench of bodily corruption or experienced a sudden and literally chilling fall in the temperature around them. Unexplained footfalls; items rearranged without any apparent agency; disembodied sighs and groans; things that go bump in the night. All these and a host of other unexplained phenomena feature in the continuous flow of reports made by people who claim to have had encounters with ghosts or other supernatural phenomena. Many of these witnesses are not suggestible, are not attention-seekers and in some cases may even be positively stolid and unimaginative. A person talking about the ghostly experiences he or she has had may incur serious ridicule. Being the butt of mockery makes most people feel uncomfortable. For this reason it is likely that many unexplained phenomena go unreported and therefore unpublicised.

Some of the stories are what might be called serial hauntings, with the same ghost being seen, heard or sensed in or around the same location by many people over a long period. Bath has one or two of these. Other ghosts have made single or at best fleeting appearances – perhaps they have completed the purpose for which they came back and, having no further business, in this world, returned whence they came. No one has ever given a fully satisfactory of why it seems that they appear to some people but not others in the same place at the same time.

The 'ghosts' may not even be the returning souls of humans. Ghostly phenomena associated with cats, dogs and horses, for example, also feature in such reports. This raises the fascinating conundrum of whether animals, like humans, can outlive their physical deaths. Some religions would consider such a claim as completely preposterous. If we accept ghostly animals as well as humans, it is worth noting that they tend to be of animals with which humans have a lot of contact and with which they can build close and often fond relationships.

Children's fictional stories may have ghosts covered in white sheets, rattling chains and emitting screeching noises. In adult fiction the ghosts are usually more subtle. In the works of that doyen of ghost story writers, M. R. James, the ghosts are little more than hints or suggestions. In spite of being so understated, they are capable of being extraordinarily menacing and malevolent. Truly the icy finger tracing out the spine.

Ghostly phenomena continue to exact a perennial interest even in the modern world dominated by the rationalities associated with the knowledge and use of science and technology; with a secular, materialist world deeply imbued with scepticism and cynicism. Even today in the twentieth century, a house reputed to be haunted may be difficult to sell. Every year priests in Britain carry out innumerable exorcisms, in all seriousness intended to bring peace to the living and repose to the spirits of the dead.

Something primeval, some vestigial sixth sense causes the tiny hairs to rise on the back of the neck at certain times and in certain places. Frissons of primeval fear verging on fright or even terror may cause a rash of goose bumps for reasons we simply cannot explain. We love mysteries and we love to be comfortably scared. Ghosts are big business. We are all fascinated by photographs or clips of film purporting to show ghostly phenomena. Films and books dealing with fictional ghosts enjoy great popularity, as do books and guided walks highlighting the paranormal phenomena of many of Britain's towns and cities. Spiritualism and psychical research are going strong and still trying to obtain incontrovertible evidence to sink the sceptics. Ghosts remain as much a part of popular culture as they were in the Middle Ages.

Do ghosts exist? If so, what are they? Do they have any objective existence or are they simply the product of superstitious minds, personal susceptibility, or overheated imagination? If we accept the claims of serious people to have had experiences of a supernatural kind, what was it they actually saw, heard or otherwise sensed? Even if we do not wish to probe too deeply into these questions, most of us can still appreciate a spooky story or movie, can keenly anticipate the thrill of jumping out of our skins or simply take pleasure in finding out about the phantoms and spectres of the place where we live. They are part of the rich and fascinating tapestry of folklore and legend that is local history.

One theory of haunting is that ghostly phenomena are a kind of spiritual film, a force generated in places where deeds of violence or great emotional upheavals have taken place. An energy is released which replicates at least some of the sights and sounds of those powerful events. This energy is then infused into the places concerned and allows the re-enactment of these events to be experienced from time to time by the still-living or at least by those people who are receptive to supernatural or psychic phenomena. If there is any substance to this theory, it does account for the eventual disappearance of some long-established ghosts. The highly charged emotional ether simply dissipates over time.

If you ask people what kinds of places they expect to be haunted, their responses would probably include 'gothic' semi-derelict mansions; the crypts of ancient churches; hoary ivy-clad old ruins; dank and dingy castle dungeons; crossroads where the bodies of highwaymen used to hang in chains suspended from gibbets, and also the local 'lovers' leap', the scene over the years of tragic suicides provoked by the miseries of unrequited love. This spiritual film idea, if anyway plausibile, helps to explain why the locations where ghosts are reported are often essentially everyday and mundane and do not fit into these categories.

The Bath district has more than its fair share of ancient buildings with historical associations and also of numerous locations boasting consistent reports of spooky happenings. However by no means do they all resemble the cliché. Some of the places and sites to be reviewed are remarkable only in their ordinariness even if the happenings associated with them are anything but ordinary. They include pubs and suburban council houses. The people who have experienced the ghostly phenomena too, are the people we would never even glance at as we pass them in the street going about their everyday business. Most are too concerned with the pressures of getting on with life in the twenty-first century to go around actively looking for paranormal experiences. Across the country as a whole, it is likely that over a third of the population will admit, perhaps a little shamefacedly, to believing in ghosts. As many as 15 per cent of the population claims to have had experiences which they thought had something to do with ghosts. The lack of scientifically gathered and verifiable evidence concerning ghosts only acts to titillate our interest and imagination. It is surely true that some honest reports of strange phenomena have unknown but entirely mundane explanations. People having powerful emotional experiences, such as terror, may not always be reliable witnesses. Some reports are made by people seeking attention and publicity – a few brief days of celebrity. Other reports come from deliberate hoaxers or those with overactive imaginations.

The Gravel Walk at night

The names of businesses and shops can change overnight. As far as possible, the names of businesses mentioned in the text were correct as at September 2008.

Finally, the author's thanks go to his son, Ed, for taking the photographs and being great company while he did so. It was hard work walking up and down all those hilly streets. His enthusiasm and support made it all worthwhile.

THREE

CENTRAL BATH

Abbey Green

Abbey Green is right in the centre of Bath and was formerly within the precincts of the Abbey. It contains a large and rather splendid tree under which there is a patch of soil in which it is said that nothing will grow. The explanation given for this curious phenomenon is that the tree was at one time used as a gallows. Although this is rather unlikely, similar stories of barren patches of earth where gallows and gibbets have previously stood are common elsewhere in Britain.

Bath Abbey

Were it not for the monstrous building in Orange Grove, opened originally as the Empire Hotel in 1899, the centre of Bath would be dominated by the Abbey. Construction work on the building to be seen today started about 1499 on the site of a much larger predecessor, the fabric of which mostly dated back to Norman times. Outwardly, Bath Abbey displays a remarkable unity of style, that known as the Perpendicular, an architectural manner unique to Britain.

The site of the Abbey has been used for religious purposes for more than a millennium and it is hardly surprising that there have been reports of supernatural phenomena in the area (see Crystal Palace, Abbey Green). There has, however, been little to report from the Abbey itself except that in the mid-1970s a tourist was taking photographs of the interior of the building. When the film was developed, he saw to his amazement the rather diaphanous figure of a monk on two of the exposures. The tourist was interested in taking pictures of architectural features, not of people, and had he seen the monk when he was lining his pictures up, he would not have taken them.

Some witnesses claim to have seen a naked monk lurking around the abbey precincts. The obvious question to ask is how could they tell he was a monk?

Battle of Lansdown

It is by no means uncommon for unexplained supernatural phenomena to be reported in and around the site of past military battles. Some experts claim that this is because of the huge

The east front of Bath Abbey

collective outburst of emotions that a battle entails. This idea certainly applies to the Battle of Lansdown on 5 July 1643.

This was an early and comparatively minor battle in the English Civil War, but for all that it was hard-fought, vicious and bloody. It was one of a number of confrontations as the two sides manoeuvred to gain control of the West Country. The location of the main engagement was on the hilly ground to the north-west of Bath. The Royalists were under the overall command of Sir Ralph Hopton, a grizzled veteran of considerable military standing who for long had been a bitter enemy of Charles I until quite inexplicably, he suddenly became an avid supporter of the King. He had around 6,500 troops at his disposal including a well-disciplined and highly effective force of Cornish infantry under Sir Beville Grenville, who valiantly led his troops from the front and in doing so, received injuries from which he later died. A monument was erected in his memory in 1720 and this can still be seen close to the road from Bath to Wick. The leader of the Parliamentary forces was the highly capable Sir William Waller. His forces consisted of about 4,500 men. He had a particularly fine troop of cavalry but the terrain over which the battle was fought did not allow the best use of this force.

The fighting started in the morning and continued sporadically all day, ranging over the hilly ground and through the abundant coverts and thickets, but with no absolute advantage being gained by either side. It eventually petered out after midnight. The Parliamentary force made a strategic withdrawal, gradually withdrawing their people and regrouping down the hill in Bath. When dawn broke, the Royalists found themselves, perhaps rather unexpectedly, in possession of the field. They were desperately short of ammunition and other supplies and could not follow up to achieve a victory. They moved off and reached Devizes a few days later whereupon they soon found themselves engaged in the Battle of Roundway Down.

Just the kind of story that would seem likely to have a ghostly outcome occurred on the morning after the battle. Some Parliamentarian prisoners were being taken from the scene of battle in an ammunition wagon. Their captors were either guilty of stupidity, neglect or misplaced humanity. Whichever applied, they allowed the prisoners to smoke. Not surprisingly, the ammunition wagon exploded, blowing the captives to smithereens just as Hopton happened to be passing. He sustained appalling injuries, losing his sight for some time and sustaining serious burns although, remarkably, he lived to fight another day.

It is disappointing to have to say that absolutely no supernatural phenomena associated with this particularly gruesome event have ever been recorded. However there are stories of strange sights and sounds associated with the battle being heard at Derwent House (q.v.), Battlefields House and Merthyr Villa, Newbridge on the western edge of Bath.

Battlefields House stands on the unclassified road climbing north out of Bath, over Lansdown towards Wick. Fighting would certainly have taken place in the vicinity during the battle. Spectral horses have been seen – perhaps they died on the field of battle – but less easy to explain are occasional sightings of two old-fashioned looking women and an aged, bent man. All three have the habit of appearing, manifesting themselves suddenly and unexpectedly, and then disappearing with equal suddenness.

In the 1960s the occupants of Merthyr Villa reported sensing the presence of a ghostly girl dressed in old-fashioned clothes. Stories have long circulated that after the battle, wounded Parliamentarian troops were treated on the site where the house now stands. Did this girl lend a hand ministering to the injured and dying? If so, why has she refused to leave the place where she did such good work? A psychic investigator gained a very strong impression of the presence of this ghost and although he did not see anything, he claimed that he knew whereabouts in the house she took her regular walks and even which windows she had a particular fondness for looking out of.

Vane Street stands on the eastern fringe of central Bath. Although the buildings in this street did not exist at the time of the Civil War, the Parliamentarian troops had used Bath as their local base and may well have had a bivouac where Vane Street now stands. It is said that annually around the anniversary of the battle the sound of jollification comes from a house in the street. The convivial sounds of jolly back-slapping, laughter, the clink of glasses and singing can be heard and are so enticing that they just invite the listener to join in. Of course this revelry might just be the present-day residents having a knees-up, but anyone with a soul and a sense of history would like to think it was the soldiers on the eve of the battle giving themselves some communal Dutch courage by trying to forget what the morrow might hold.

Beehive, Belvedere

The first reports of supernatural phenomena in this pub date from the 1970s. On a number of occasions an apparition described as looking like an old-fashioned female domestic servant was seen. Apparently middle-aged, she was meticulously turned out in a black uniform, a starched and brilliantly white apron, a little cap and black shoes which were so well polished that had she chosen to do so, she could have used them as a mirror. Her appearances were quite fleeting. She materialised as if from nowhere although always either in the hall or one of the bedrooms, stood for a few seconds and then seemingly melted out of sight. Not the least curious aspect of all this was that although she disappeared from the sight of the human witnesses, she clearly remained visible to the pub dog. His head and eye movements showed that he was following her around the room. Dogs are known for an ability to sense the presence of something not always perceptible to humans and they frequently growl, while their hackles also rise and they bare their teeth. With this apparition, however, the dog showed no signs of either fear or anger. This matched the response the ghost evoked in the humans. All who saw it made it clear that they did not feel threatened in any way.

She appeared literally on and off, and those who saw her almost came to regard her as part of the family, giving her the affectionate nickname of 'Bunty'. Not only did she materialise from time to time in the way described but her unseen presence was indicated by the lids being lifted off pans and then carefully replaced, sometimes when they were on the cooker and food was being prepared. It was if she was checking just to make sure everything was in order, just as a conscientious servant would do.

In the 1990s there were there was a repetition of supernatural phenomena, with reports of the opening and closing of doors and of sudden feelings of intense cold. Some explained this in terms of the ghost of a man who had hanged himself on the premises. Rumours used to circulate that the ghosts of soldiers coming back from the Battle of Lansdown were sometimes to be seen trudging past the pub. Alternatively and perhaps as the result of the consumption of even more copious quantities of strong cider, the marching ghostly soldiers have been described as Roman Legionaries.

This pub has undergone a transformation and is now called Grappa's Bar, clearly aiming for a different clientele.

Belvedere

'Belvedere' is the name given to a part of the west side of Lansdown Road, just past its junction with Montpelier and not far out of the city centre. Many years ago a house in Belvedere was the scene of a horrible haunting. Two small children, a boy and a girl, were occupying an upstairs bedroom. Their parents were downstairs when suddenly they jumped out of their skins as the peace of the evening was shattered by an ear-piercing scream. Mother and father rushed upstairs to find the children clutching each other in terror and sitting on a piece of rolled up carpet which, half-an-hour ago when their parents had turned-off the light, had been laid out in the normal way. The children managed to blurt out that they had been lying in their respective beds in the dark when there had been what they described as a 'rattling' noise. They had jumped out of bed and, shaking with fear, for some reason or other instead of doing the obvious thing which was to make for the door, they had sat down on the roll of carpet. Nor, oddly, did they then call out. However, when there was a crunching, shattering sound as of splintering wood both children screamed, giving it all they had got. Their parents arrived in the room seconds later. The top had been ripped off a wardrobe which had only been bought a few weeks previously. No explanation was ever given for how the carpet came to be rolled up or the wardrobe damaged but the children not surprisingly refused to sleep in the room again. Such a feeling of tension developed in the house that it was decided to perform an exorcism. Whether this was efficacious or quite simply that whatever caused these phenomena had simply expunged all its malevolent energy on the carpet and the wardrobe will never be known, but nothing untoward has happened since.

Bennett Street

Bennett Street runs between The Circus and Landsdown Road just north of the city centre. No. 19 Bennett Street is allegedly haunted by the ghost of Admiral Arthur Phillip (1738–1814).

He was in command of the 'First Fleet' as the convoy of ships taking the initial batch of convicted felons to New South Wales was known. The convicts' death sentences had been commuted to transportation and they were despatched to the furthest corner of the planet in a prime example of an 'out of sight, out of mind' attitude on the part of the authorities. Phillip's brief was to establish a penal colony at Botany Bay as a preliminary to further settlement at a later stage. He was also to act as the first Governor of the colony. Phillip was an efficient administrator as well as a humane and compassionate man which helps to account for his high standing in the annals of Australian history. It is not surprising that the conditions at Botany Bay took their toll of his health and he returned to England a very sick man. He recovered and went back to active service, eventually reaching the rank of Rear Admiral of the Blue. One account says that he committed suicide in the house.

Unfortunately the author has been unable to locate much information about the alleged haunting at No. 19. The lack of stories suggests that if his spirit does indeed remain on the premises, it is like him, quiet, efficient and self-effacing. It seems that he has been seen dressed in old-fashioned civilian clothes and sitting in front of the fire in one of the downstairs rooms at the back of the house. He tends to fade away when spoken to. Those who claim to have seen this figure describe him, a trifle unkindly, as 'ugly'. The author would be very grateful to any reader who could supply information about this elusive haunting.

Bennett Street

Gateway of Bewdley House

Bewdley House, off Prior Park Road

This sizeable Victorian villa stands in extensive grounds and in the 1930s and 1940s it gained the reputation of being haunted. The most frequently seen phenomenon was apparently the ghost of a woman wearing a blue dress and a bonnet from which curly tresses peeped rather coyly. Her face was distinguished by a long nose and thin cheeks and when she appeared, which was only ever fleetingly, she seemed to be stooped or to be dragging something, not visible to the observer's eye, across the floor.

Sometimes those in the house experienced a sudden extreme chill even on a day of extreme heat and this was said to be associated with the ghost of an old man who was himself never seen. This phenomenon was disconcerting, but not so as much as the sound of scratching outside bedrooms at night, as if someone or something was impotently trying to open the door. Those inside the rooms were only too glad that whatever it was did not manage to gain entrance.

Broad Street

Broad Street, slightly north of Bath city centre, is narrow and congested with traffic. In the mid-1970s there were reports that a flat at No. 17 was haunted. A number of phenomena were experienced in a short period before the place went back to its pre-spooky slumbers. The occupants heard the clink of glasses coming from the kitchen as if a convivial time was being had in there. Investigation of the kitchen revealed nothing untoward but one of the occupants said that he saw a tall, cowled figure disappearing upstairs. This figure was seen a few more times over the following weeks. A few sharp knocking sounds were also heard but this activity subsided and apparently there has been no repetition.

No. 10 Burlington Street

Burlington Street runs up the steep lower slopes of Landsdown Hill, north of the city centre. Back in the 1920s, this building was the vicarage for Christ Church which was close by. There was a brief flurry of almost frenzied paranormal activity. A child with long hair put in an appearance, as did an elderly woman thought to be the wife of a previous vicar, and a man equipped with a wooden leg who seemed to take great delight in stumping around the attic during the hours of darkness, keeping the occupants awake. The phenomena ceased as suddenly as they had started. Nothing else is recorded. Could it be that the premises were being renovated? Reports of ghostly activity where none have previously been made often follow after demolitions or structural alterations, as if the spirits in the fabric have been disturbed and have emerged to see what is going on, and perhaps to show ways of expressing their displeasure.

Camden Crescent

Camden Crescent stands close to the northern part of Bath city centre. A house in the crescent offers up an occasional sighting of a ghost. It is supposed to be that of a long-standing family servant who, in the early nineteenth century, was shot dead as he tried to intervene in a heated quarrel over cards between his master and a man who made his profession from playing (and cheating) at cards. No wonder then that he has been described as very sad-faced. From time to time, people claim to have seen such a figure gazing forlornly from a window in the frontage of the house.

Camden Crescent

Above: Beckford's Bridge, Lansdown Crescent

Left: Beckford's Plaque

Cameley Green, Twerton

Twerton is a suburb to the west of Bath. In the 1970s the lives of a family in an otherwise unexceptional house in an equally unexceptional street in Twerton were made a misery by what was described as a 'phantom with horrible wrinkled skin'. The spectre made its debut on three successive nights, manifesting itself to the woman of the house who was in bed in the middle of the night. The first night was bad enough. The woman woke up, her heart palpitating and in a cold sweat and then spent the rest of the night tossing and turning, reliving the horrors of what she thought had been a particularly intense nightmare. When the vision reappeared on the following two nights, all she could do was scream, thrash about in the bed for a few seconds and then, thankfully, pass out. By this time she knew it was no mere nightmare.

Her experience obviously disturbed and alarmed the rest of the household. The ghost, however, perhaps pleased by the effect it seemed to have had on the woman, then decided to try its luck with others in the family. It appeared before a young woman who was nursing her baby in the middle of the night. It showed that it had other tricks up its sleeve by causing a picture on the wall to swing to and fro with the intensity of a windscreen wiper. This spectacular effect was accompanied by a chilling fall in the temperature. First described as about 5ft high and looking rather like a pile of washing, on its repeated manifestations, those who saw it modified their description and called it 'the creature with the horrible wrinkled skin'.

The effect on the householders was traumatic. Whatever it was continued to make occasional appearances over the next fortnight and the family were left with little alternative but to hand in their notice – some of them were already receiving medical attention for stress. An attempted exorcism seems only to have made things worse. Not surprisingly these events made the news and the house became vacant, for a while it was the council's most wanted property. Those who moved in later had no weird experiences and as is the way with such things, the case soon became yesterday's news.

The idea of a ghost with a face like a pile of washing will ring a bell with aficionados of M. R. James, perhaps the doyen of English ghost story writers. In his chilling and atmospheric story, '*Oh whistle and I'll come to you, my lad*', the thing that scares a rather prim professor absolutely witless was remembered by him as having 'a horrible, an intensely horrible, face of crumpled linen'.

Charles Street

This street reverberates to the din of the incessant traffic which skirts the west side of the city centre. The Registry Office is located in Charles Street and was formerly the location for a regular spooky phenomenon. Every Thursday at exactly 10.30A.M., a tapping would be heard on one specific outer door. The building once housed a private local bank whose owner in 1888 was an Ebenezer Ash. Another account says that he was a bank porter. He himself lived on the premises but had a fall, went into a long-lasting coma and died without recovering. It was reckoned that it was Ash's ghost that did the rapping. No one ever explained why 10.30A.M. on Thursday morning clearly meant so much to the old chap, or rather, to his ghost.

Former Christopher Hotel

Some hoteliers reckon that having a known ghost on the premises is bad for business. Others believe that it boosts trade. There was certainly a room in the Christopher Hotel from which reports regularly used to come in about unexplained, possibly supernatural activity. These have included comments to the effect that guests felt that they were being watched by invisible, disapproving eyes; that the room had a spooky feeling; and that occasionally the temperature would suddenly drop, creating an unpleasant icy chill. Several guests claimed that something tugged their bed clothes off in the middle of the night. One guest complained because he thought he had got lucky with someone wanting to share his bed because his duvet fell to the floor, whereupon he put the light on and was greatly disappointed to find no one there. There wasn't much the management could do about that.

The Christopher was one of a clutch of three important old inns that formerly stood in High Street. It was located on the corner with Cheap Street, and the building is now used for other purposes.

No.13 The Circus

The basement flat at No.13 made something of a name for itself in the late 1950s and early 1960s. It is claimed that it was the scene of a haunting by a woman wearing a long grey dress. Before the occupier who had the supernatural experiences moved in, renovation work was done on the flat and the workmen involved had commented on the eerie and threatening atmosphere. They were convinced that the place was haunted and they commented wryly that they wouldn't want to spend the night there – a comment that must have done little for the confidence of the lady who was about to move in. No sooner was she installed than there was an outbreak of classic poltergeist activity. The lady was a naturally tidy person and therefore disconcerted and understandably more than a little irritated when things that she had carefully arranged would be found scattered around in other parts of the flat. Obviously she must have been quite fastidious because she took to drawing chalk circles round objects on flat surfaces just to make sure that these items had actually been moved and that it was not just her imagination. When she went back to look at them, sometimes they had moved no more than a few centimetres. On other occasions they had been mysteriously been transported to other rooms.

There were other manifestations as well. The leaves of pot plants would sway as if in a breeze, despite the fact that all the doors and windows were closed. The occupant woke up at night on several occasions hearing someone moving round the room, but she never saw anything that could have been responsible for the sound. The woman who came in to do her cleaning was adamant that she *had* seen something, and this on several occasions. What she saw was an elderly woman sitting by the fire, wearing a long dress. She had never summoned the courage to address this spectre. It may have been the ghost of a long-deceased servant.

A general view of The Circus

Crown Inn, Bathwick Street

Crown Inn, Bathwick Street

Bathwick Street, just on the north-eastern fringe of the city centre, heaves with traffic day and night. In the early 1990s there were several reports from bar staff and customers that a ghostly figure, looking like a First World War soldier, had been seen sitting in a dark corner supping his ale from what appeared to be a pewter tankard. Significantly, many troops were stationed in this part of the city during the First World War. What is the explanation? He doesn't seem to have stayed as one of the regulars for long. Could it be that he died in the vicinity but that demolition or rebuilding work was being carried out on buildings he was familiar with nearby and this disturbed his spirit? Such work often seems to disturb the dead and leads to sometimes very short-lived outbreaks of haunting.

Crystal Palace, Abbey Green

Right in the centre of Bath stands the Crystal Palace pub. There has been a pub on this site for centuries. The present building was once known as The Three Tuns, undergoing its change of name in the middle of the nineteenth century to commemorate the Great Exhibition of 1851. This was held in Hyde Park in London and housed in a striking and innovative prefabricated building of glass and iron designed by Joseph Paxton. It received the affectionate and admiring nickname 'Crystal Palace' when an enterprising journalist saw it just after a heavy shower of rain followed by a burst of sunlight when it literally glistened like crystal. The name caught on.

The pub stands on the site of a Roman building, and renovation work about thirty years ago revealed a splendid Roman tessellated pavement. No Roman ghosts have manifested themselves, but the pub occasionally hosts a figure with hood and cowl, which is taken to be the ghost of a monk. Bath Abbey is an immensely impressive building which dominates the centre of the city, but it is something of a misnomer to call it an 'abbey'. A church existed on the site possibly as early as the seventh century and it became a Benedictine abbey around AD 963. It was only

Crystal Palace   Dead Mill, Larkhall

an abbey until 1090 when it became a cathedral priory and as such it was dissolved in 1540. Almost the entire fabric of the present 'abbey' dates from a radical reconstruction which began in 1499. Large though that building is, the earlier conventual buildings would have been far more extensive and Abbey Green may have been within the precincts. This may help to explain the mystery figure of the monk. Although sightings have been made over many years, it put in a number of appearances during the rebuilding work which unearthed the Roman pavement. Reports of ghosts frequently coincide with such building or excavation work as if the spirits are disturbed, perhaps even resentful, that their normal routine is being so rudely disrupted. One of the ghost's favourite activities is to make empty glasses rattle. When this happens, do the knees knock of all those within earshot?

Dead Mill, Larkhall

Larkhall is a suburb to the north-east of Bath city centre. Over the years there have been a number of reports of the sound of heavy, slow footsteps treading with great deliberation on the wooden floors upstairs in this old and much-altered building. Such phenomena are not uncommon but what makes them different here is that the only people who hear them seem to be visitors to the building. Explain that one!

Derwent House, Kelston Road

It is said that in an earlier house on this site, a military surgeon lived who attempted, without success, to save the life of the Royalist Sir Beville Grenville, who was brought from the scene of the fighting at Landsown in 1643 having sustained appalling injuries in the battle. In this area of Bath, as well as the neighbouring Weston district, there have been over the years many reports of the sounds of jingling harness', the neighing of horses, the clatter of horseshoes and the appearance of riderless horses, just the kind of thing that might be expected in the aftermath of a battle. For readers who really want something sensational, the author can only apologise and anticipate their disappointment when he has to say that these are not headless horses. The equine noises, however, had sufficient substance to cause Georgian and Victorian occupants of the house to run down to the stables to make sure that all was well with their horses.

The ghost of the old-fashioned girl said to haunt Merthyr Villa is also said to have been seen at Derwent House.

Devonshire Arms, Wellsway

Wellsway forms part of the busy A367 as it makes its way southwards out of Bath. The Devonshire Arms hit the local news in 1996 when there were reports of a ghost at large in the cellar. Doors that had been firmly bolted mysteriously opened, items stored in the cellar tidily were moved or thrown around by an invisible hand, and a thermometer snapped in two for no very obvious reason. Those concerned agreed that it was the ghost of a nineteenth-century girl, killed in a railway accident.

Devonshire Arms

Edward Street

Edward Street

Edward Street runs between Great Pulteney Street and the northern end of Pulteney Road on the eastern fringe of the city centre. The buildings of which this street is composed are mostly divided into flats, and in one of these flats it was reckoned that there was an annual occurrence of the sound of dancing on wooden floors to the accompaniment of stately old world music, a strange phenomenon. These sounds apparently moved around the flat which consisted of several rooms, but stopped abruptly if a certain door was opened.

Garrick's Head, Saw Close

This building right in the city centre was erected about 1720 and it became the home of Richard 'Beau' Nash (1674-1762) who not only lived there for twenty years but used it as a smart gambling club for the rich but louche and raffish set with whom he liked to while away the time. He himself was a compulsive gambler. The Garrick's Head has been a pub for many years.

The building has attracted many ghost stories. One is that a murder took place on the premises when a cuckolded husband who had discovered that his wife was conducting an affair, found himself sitting at the gambling table close to the man he knew to be his wife's lover. Suddenly overcome by insane jealousy, he is supposed to have unsheathed his sword and attempted to run the man through the heart. Apparently he missed the heart but he nevertheless succeeded in his intention to kill the man who was a rival for his wife's passionate embraces. If he thought that the death of the lover might lead to a happy reconciliation with his wife, he was badly mistaken. As soon as she heard of her paramour's death, she rushed to the scene, shaking and weeping hysterically with tears coursing down her face. Obviously she was something of a drama queen for she then screamed imprecations of hatred aimed at her husband who was absent, undoubtedly already helping the authorities with their enquiries. She followed this display up by rather melodramatically leaping out of the window, thereby either intentionally or otherwise managing to commit suicide and get her name in the papers. Such an outburst of emotions involving a murder and a suicide in a brief, concentrated period may well have created enough psychic energy to explain the occasional scream as the ghost of the demented woman relives her grief and her fatal fall. Her lover, not unnaturally, is also said to be present on these occasions but he remains silent.

The Garrick's Head has been the location of many reports of poltergeist activity over the years. Poltergeists are frequently described as 'mischievous' but they are known on occasions to be more sinister and threatening, acting in a decidedly malicious and violent fashion. Although unseen they can certainly be noisy. Indeed the word 'poltergeist' means something like 'noisy spirit'. They are seemingly responsible for disembodied aural effects, such as knocking, banging and rapping, but they are probably best known for their seeming ability to move objects around with no visible agency, and for turning electrical apparatus on and off. This activity may take the form of nothing more harmful than the movement of a letter or similar light object a few inches or feet, although even this can obviously be disconcerting. Far more alarming is the inexplicable movement of much larger and heavier objects over longer distances. In extreme cases, and this is where the malice really seems to click in, objects have seemingly been launched by an invisible hand and aimed at vulnerable parts of the human anatomy such as the head. Those who study such paranormal manifestations describe this phenomenon as 'pyschokinesis'.

Garrick's
Head pub

A curious point about poltergeists is that, unlike most ghosts, they seem to prefer to do their tricks when there is an audience. It also seems that the presence of certain people can initiate the activities of an otherwise quiescent poltergeist – teenage children for example. The spirit of the Garrick's Head has manifested itself innumerable times over the decades unlike most poltergeists whose activity is generally short-lived. This mischievous spirit has moved light items such as bunches of keys, sometimes simply a few yards away, but at other times secreting them in unexpected places. Items such as candles have been moved before the very gaze of horrified onlookers and, worst of all, a heavy old-fashioned cash register was removed from the top of the bar and hurled across the room with such force as to smash a chair which got in the way. Compared with this violence, wall cupboards shaking for no obvious reason, money going missing only to reappear days later in rooms that were normally locked and that no one had been into, and the invisible switching off of electrical apparatus were quite tame. Even the sound of the toilet being flushed when nobody is in there is just odd rather than something to get frightened about. At least someone, perhaps the ghost, has been relieved.

It is not uncommon for pub cellars to have an unpleasant, even threatening atmosphere. The cellar at the Garrick's Head is no exception. Over the years there have been many reports that members of staff working in the cellars have felt that they were not alone and were unnerved by the feeling that their every move was being watched by invisible and unfriendly eyes. The cellar itself always seems much colder than even a pub cellar should be. Items have been moved about by unseen hands. One licensee was using a mallet to drive wooden bungs into beer casks when he was suddenly called upstairs. He returned to the cellar only a few moments later to find that the mallet had disappeared. He never did find it, despite the fact that no one else could possibly have gone down into the cellar in the short time he was away.

What is now the Garrick's Head pub is next door to the Theatre Royal. The actor, David Garrick (1717-1779) was among the later tenants when the building was still used for residential purposes. To save him the bother of having to step out into the street, he had a doorway made through the party wall into the adjacent theatre. On occasions a figure dressed in clothes of the Regency period and sporting a large wig has been seen making its way through the door from the pub into the theatre. Also frequently sensed is a strong sweet but attractive smell, like that of jasmine. This smell, which occurs in the cellar and elsewhere in the pub, is thought to be evidence of the ghost of a woman who is said to have hanged herself in one of the bedrooms. She was apparently the prize to be won in a duel between two men, one of whom she loved but who was run through with a sword, sustaining injuries from which he quickly died. Quite how she agreed to become party to such a duel has never been established but her continued presence on the premises is thought to be because her remorse will not let her rest in peace.

Yet another ghost who has been reported is that of a lady in grey who is usually seen in the theatre next door but who clearly likes an occasional change of scenery. She is also supposed to have committed suicide by jumping out of one of the windows. Those who take their own lives are traditionally thought of as finding it very hard to experience peace or rest after their deaths, and a great many ghost stories concern suicides. Some people believe that it is the lady in grey who produces the aroma of jasmine.

Is it the ghosts or the resident poltergeists that are responsible for the disturbed nights that guests who stay in the pub's bedrooms often complain about? Some of these guests are working in performances in the theatre and may be in residence for several weeks. Although they seem eventually to get used to the idiosyncrasies of the place, there have been many reports of knockings on doors in the dark hours of the night, menacing footsteps over creaking floorboards, door handles turning when there is apparently no one there to turn them and sinister, mirthless laughs.

Guest bedroom No.3 has the reputation of being haunted. A guest sleeping in the room for several nights woke in horror each night with the sensation of what he described as 'rope burns' on his neck. We can only admire his fortitude at having undergone this ordeal on a number of occasions without requesting a change of room. It could hardly have helped when he was informed that in the late eighteenth century a woman committed suicide by hanging in that very room. Still, he had a tale to tell his grandchildren.

A bust of Garrick

Gay Street

Gay Street is a hill leading up to one of Bath's greatest architectural gems – The Circus. The word 'gay' has long meant carefree, blithe or merry although it is currently used less and less in this sense. In nineteenth-century slang it was used to refer to what were euphemistically known as 'ladies of the night'. Later slang usage had the expression 'to feel gay' which meant to be amorously-inclined. Alternatively, 'gay' could be used simply to describe a person who was sexually active. 'Gaying it' meant copulation. 'Gay' gained its new accepted meaning relatively recently. While researching this book, the author came across the report that a homosexual ghost had been seen in Gay Street. This sounds like a not very subtle leg-pull. Even if a ghost was observed roaming this street, one question immediately comes to mind. How did the witness know that it was homosexual? Others have jumped on the bandwagon and claim that this ghost has his hair tied back, perhaps in a pony tail.

At No.8, which was once the home of Mrs Thrale, a friend of the immortal Dr Johnson, one of the reception rooms was haunted. The sound of conversation could be heard apparently in another room close by. If the door to that room was opened, the hubbub ceased abruptly.

Another house on the other side of Gay Street was occupied as a local headquarters by the American military police during the Second World War. Great brawny six-footers with crew-cuts, bulging biceps, bull-like necks and prognathous jaws were turned into whimpering wimps who could not bear to be alone in the building, and all this by an unspecified but infinitely menacing 'presence'.

Gay Street takes its name from a Dr Robert Gay who owned the land on which it was built.

Gravel Walk

The Gravel Walk forms a delightful pedestrian promenade between the Royal Victoria Park and the city centre. It has a ghost, reported to be a tall man with white hair protruding from under his hat. He is said to resemble an elderly well-to-do gentleman of the nineteenth century. Those who claim to have seen him, and they are many over the years, have found him mysterious but not menacing. Some of them, however, have been a little put out by his apparent ability to walk through objects, including humans, in his path. Equally strange is the fact that he evidently cannot be seen by all those using the Gravel Walk because observers say that they have seen people simply passing straight through him, obviously completely unaware of his presence.

Some years ago a lady walked to her workplace in Milsom Street after leaving her car in Victoria Park. She did this every day of the working week and she used to make her way into the city centre along the Gravel Walk. This was a pleasant experience tempered only by the fact that she was, after all, going to work. However on one particular day, she had an experience that she would never forget…

She was walking along briskly when she became aware of someone close behind her on her left side. This naturally made her feel uncomfortable and this feeling was compounded by the fact that she hadn't heard the person's footsteps on the gravel. She hurried her pace but the figure which she could discern out of the corner of her eye accelerated too. She described him as male and dressed predominantly in grey. Few people were about and she was feeling distinctly uneasy about this ill-mannered man on her shoulder when, in her words, he suddenly 'went through her', leaving her trembling on her knees and feeling as if her body had been sapped of all its strength. Her workmates were extremely concerned when she turned up, shaking and ashen-faced, and she poured out her story, telling them that she had just seen a ghost. One of them didn't seem particularly surprised and asked exactly where it had happened. It had been near the dip in the Gravel Walk and her workmate told her that this particular spot was haunted because, long ago, judicial hangings had taken place there.

About a year later she had another weird experience, although there does not seem to have been any connection between them. She was busily engaged massaging a customer. He was partly disabled and not given to saying very much but on this occasion he told her that in a past life he had been hanged for theft. This was a strange thing to come out with suddenly, but even more peculiar he told her that he distinctly remembered her from this previous life, having frequently noted her when he was walking along Brock Street which runs from the Royal Crescent to The Circus.

Left: The Gravel Walk facing west

Below: The Gravel Walk facing east

No.20 Henrietta Street

No.20 Henrietta Street

Henrietta Road and Henrietta Street run between Bathwick and Laura Place on the east side of the Avon. At No.20 the ghost of Admiral Robinson (1722-1799) appears from time to time. Those on the floor beneath can here him treading ponderously across the room and then ascending the stairs whereupon the sounds stop abruptly. It should come as no surprise that many old sea dogs dropped anchor in Bath for their last years. Many were very rich men who were attracted by the social life of the city when it was at its most fashionable. Later, when Bath was relatively in the doldrums, its atmosphere attracted others who would perhaps best be described as 'shabby genteel'.

A house in the street has a room with a stain on the hearthstone which cannot be removed no matter how much old-fashioned elbow grease is applied. It even refuses to succumb to the application of any number of modern 'miracle' stain removers. It is supposedly the blood of a woman who was beaten into a pulp by her husband who then left her for dead, spread-eagled in this very spot. Chemical analysis would probably reveal that the stain in the stone is produced by a trace of iron oxide. However books about ghosts would not arouse the interest they do if those who wrote them produced cold, scientific and objective explanations for all strange supernatural or paranormal phenomena.

Holloway

Holloway huddles under the precipice of Beechen Cliff, south of the city centre and just across the River Avon. For centuries Holloway formed the main approach road to Bath from the south-west. Here in medieval times the Benedictine Order of monks had a hospice or perhaps a 'lazar house' where they ministered to lepers, an aspect of the work of the monastic orders which is often forgotten.

A number of houses in Holloway stand on parts of the site of the former Benedictine establishment. One of them had a resident poltergeist in the 1960s and 1970s which was given the familiar name of 'Charlie', although by no means entirely out of affection. Charlie engaged in all the types of activity associated with his kind, few of which were really terrifying but all of which were disconcerting and some just downright infuriating. Windows which had been firmly closed would be found inexplicably open, letting in the rain or the cold, while those left open for a good reason would be shut by invisible hands. Pictures and ornaments on the walls would be glimpsed being moved about without evident agency and small objects like coins and keys would be thrown across the room although never, seemingly, with intent to injure. As might be expected, disembodied knockings and rappings took place and, perhaps needless to say, door handles rattled or were turned unwontedly and a wide range of household objects disappeared only to turn up unexpectedly elsewhere on the premises, sometimes months after the occupants had resentfully given them up for lost. The malicious spirit seemed to reserve a particular hatred for Christmas decorations. Once they had been put up, it seemed to derive great pleasure from pulling them down and scattering them around the room.

The Gothic Cottage, Holloway

The former chapel of the leper colony

Charlie however did have one trick up his sleeve which marked him out from all those run-of-the-mill poltergeists. When the whim took him, he teleported the resident cat! Tiddles, Pussikins or whatever the cat was called, had settled down by the fire, luxuriating in that sensuous way that cats do in a source of heat, when he would find himself carried some distance by an invisible force and then gently put back down to earth, unharmed physically but probably a long way from the fire and definitely out of his comfort zone. Doubtless Tiddles then stalked off in that dignified and supercilious way that cats have as if to say he wouldn't allow himself to be inconvenienced even if somebody had nothing better to do than to want to play silly buggers with him!

Another supernatural presence seen many years ago was the figure of an avuncular looking man dressed in clothes of the Tudor period.

Since then there have been occasional reports of the sighting of ghosts and of unexplained mists often accompanied by sudden and very marked drops in temperature, but as with all reports of such phenomena, these need to be taken with a pinch of salt, otherwise known as the exercising of healthy scepticism.

Kensington Place

Kensington Place is on the south side of London Road just out of the city centre. A strange story from the nineteenth century concerns the visit of a lady to a house in this vicinity. She described the house as having been built in the eighteenth century and giving off an old-fashioned feel. She visited on the very best kind of English summer's day – bright and sunny and warm but with just a slight breeze to temper the heat. The garden looked an absolute treat with a trim well-kept lawn and a mass of gorgeous old English traditional garden flowers.

Although she had never actually visited the house before, she knew the occupants well. They were elderly ladies and she was making a long-promised social call. The lady guest and her hosts sat by the open French windows, peacefully, almost soporifically, drinking in the idyllic scene before them and engaged in a lazy, rather sporadic conversation. The visitor, however, found her attention increasingly being drawn to a marble fountain. This was in the form of a satyr which stood, perhaps a little precariously, on one leg, its other leg being splayed out apparently for balance. Involuntarily and certainly against her natural instincts, her eyes kept returning to the face of this satyr. It bore an expression that could only be described as one of sheer diabolical malevolence.

Try as she might, and despite the pleasantries being exchanged with her charming friends, she could not wrest her mind away from this grotesque garden ornament, so out of keeping with the charm of its tranquil surroundings. Visitors and guest continued to sit, to ruminate and to swap desultory comments for another hour or two until they all agreed that it was getting rather chilly. The lady visitor's comment was that it had become cold extraordinarily quickly. The wind had an icy edge to it.

The group continued to sit and exchange small talk but now with the French windows closed. Our visitor's drifting attention was suddenly riveted when the French windows opened and through them came a figure she described as 'the quaintest old lady in a crinoline and starched stomacher and wearing a high poke bonnet'. In her hand she had a garden trowel. Her face was a mask of malice and hate reminiscent of the satyr.

Her hostesses made no sign to acknowledge the newcomer's presence or even that they were aware of her presence. This was curious enough in itself but then even stranger and more disconcerting was the fact that when the old lady crossed in front of the mirror, she cast no reflection!

In due course the old lady re-crossed the room, opened the French windows, passed through and closed them behind her. She then walked across the garden and disappeared behind a hedge of yew, beautifully cared for like the rest of the garden. Our lady visitor was more mystified than frightened and so, casually, she asked her hostesses who was the lady in old-fashioned clothes who had come and gone through the French windows. She began to doubt her own sanity when they made it clear that there was no old-fashioned lady. No one had come and gone, they asserted firmly, although they were clearly somewhat put out to hear what their guest thought she had witnessed.

Confused, fascinated and not a little frightened, the visitor clearly possessed a dogged nature. Not being prepared to let the matter drop and wanting to satisfy her own curiosity, she decided to look into the matter further. She discovered that the house had the reputation of being haunted by the ghost of a singularly unpleasant and curmudgeonly old fellow who had lived there in the reign of George III (1760-1820). It was said that he had amassed a huge fortune in money and valuables which he buried in his garden for safe keeping. Unfortunately for him, when he came to recover the hoard, he couldn't find it. Perhaps it had been stolen but whatever the explanation, try as he might, he never did recover it and the frustration and anxiety caused by this loss was said to have driven him insane.

This was all very interesting but hardly germane to the task of finding out about the lady in the poke-bonnet. However, continued research revealed that other people had indeed reported seeing her and it was clear that those who had done so had always been visitors. The house gained something of a blighted reputation and was often 'To Let' because most would-be tenants did not wish to live in a house with the reputation of being haunted. Sod's Law dictated that those who took on the tenancy precisely because they hoped to see the ghost, of course, never did so.

Kensington Place

Left: Ghostly keystone on former Gorvesnor Hotel

Below: The former Grosvenor Hotel

In the vicinity is another dwelling containing a ghost commonly known as 'Lady Betty'. It is claimed that this ghost is that of a former young lady of the house, heir to the family fortune. She was foolish enough to fall in love with one of the servants, a groom, and then indiscreet enough to be interrupted in the course of trying to elope with him. Her father, who caught them red-handed, was notoriously short-tempered. He was a large man and he aimed a vicious blow at the despised groom but missed and hit his daughter instead. He did so with such force that he knocked her down the front steps of the house and she landed badly, breaking her neck and dying shortly afterwards. 'Lady Betty' has been described as a middle-aged lady in grey, a description which does not accord with the age of the unfortunate young woman accidentally dispatched to her death by her exceptionally irascible father. A cynic might say that the experience had clearly aged her.

Beckford's Tower, Lansdown

What can be said about William Beckford and his imposing edifice on a relatively flat piece of terrain surrounded on all sides by steep hills, a couple of miles north of Bath? Little perhaps except that at this stage the tower at Lansdown is a considerably scaled-down version of the much loftier tower he built some distance away at Fonthill in Wiltshire.

William Beckford (1759-1844) was a man who has always attracted attention and a plethora of stories, many of them inevitably apocryphal. He is a natural item for inclusion in any anthology of English eccentrics. At the age of about eleven he inherited the family fortune, worth many millions of pounds, which was based on his father's ownership of sugar plantations in the Caribbean. His father was a serial philanderer who fathered innumerable illegitimate offspring. Unlike them, Beckford, described at ten years of age as being 'wilful, petulant and possessed of an unbridled temper', had already shown a certain feminine and artistic delicacy and was more interested in classical music, literature and the arts than in physical roistering and skylarking with other boys. They thought he was what used to be described as a 'pansy' but he didn't seem to care. His dominating mother tried to develop his machismo by sending him on the Grand Tour but this only seemed to whet his appetite for learning about foreign cultural achievements rather than appreciating the opportunity for casual sexual encounters, duels and monster drinking bouts, which were the expected pleasures of young English gentlemen while doing the European circuit. He incurred the ridicule and contempt of his social peers when he expressed his revulsion with blood sports. He never forgave them for the derision they poured on his likes and dislikes.

Beckford's millions made him one of the country's most eligible bachelors and he was assailed wherever he went by importunate mothers lining him up for matrimony with their daughters. On a tour of grand English country houses to which his riches inevitably gave him the entrée, he visited Powderham Castle in Devon and promptly fell head-over-heels in love with William Courtenay, known as 'Kitty', who was just eleven years of age and the future Earl of Devon. With his usual disregard for opinion, Beckford made no secret of his passion. The wife of his cousin then became infatuated with Beckford and in order to become close to him, she apparently even agreed to act as a go-between in his affair with young Courtenay. Salaciously, it has been hinted that they all went to bed in a bizarre ménage-a-trois.

Beckford was probably bisexual and the experience described above did not prevent him making a socially advantageous marriage in 1783 to the delightful, pretty and gifted Lady Margaret Gordon, daughter of the Duke of Hamilton. They had two children. She seemingly accepted his sexual proclivities and forgave them, attempting to give him the support his somewhat fragile personality needed. When she died just three years later, he was grief-stricken and this, combined with the social ostracism he suffered as a result of the publicity surrounding his ongoing affair with Courtenay, led him to became embittered, brooding, lonely and introspective. Homosexual activity was still a capital offence and although his wealth and social position probably accounted for the fact that he was never prosecuted for it, he decided to leave England and live abroad, which he did for more than a decade.

In Europe he led an extraordinary peripatetic existence, accompanied by an entourage which included his own trusted doctor, valet, baker, chef, three faithful footmen, a troupe of no fewer than twenty-four musicians and his personal favourite, a Spanish, although some say an Italian, dwarf. This dwarf is reputed to have existed on an exclusive diet of mushrooms. All Beckford's attendants are said to have been homosexual although this may have been a malicious rumour. Also with him were two much-loved dogs which rejoiced respectively in the names of 'Mrs Fry' and 'Viscount Fartleberry'. His riches were such that he was invited to visit the castles and mansions of many eminent European families. Beckford was extremely cultured and learned and he could be delightfully charming company when he chose. However he offended his hosts on many occasions by his insistence that, while accepting their hospitality, he would supply his own plates, cutlery and bed-linen. More irksome, even unforgivable, was his habit of wallpapering the guest bedrooms in which he slept even if they already had high quality wallpaper in perfect condition. This was unceremoniously removed by his people and his choice of wall covering substituted.

Beckford's grave

Perhaps Beckford's rootless urge to tour declined as he got older because in his late thirties he returned to England and embarked on the enterprise for which he will always be remembered, even if all his other activities had faded away in the mists of time. His main country estate was at Fonthill Gifford in south-west Wiltshire, fifteen miles west of Salisbury and it consisted of 4,900 acres. It was beautifully landscaped and contained a fine and opulent Palladian mansion known as 'Fonthill Splendens'. This had replaced earlier houses on the same site and Beckford moved in. However, he had a low opinion of Fonthill Splendens and he decided to build a new home on a hill, half-a-mile to the west. He employed James Wyatt, a member of a highly-regarded dynasty of architects to draw up a design in which he himself had a considerable input.

What evolved was a loose interpretation of a large medieval Gothic monastery, a cruciform-shaped complex of buildings designed to be an impressive and sumptuous home and dominated by a tower between 275 and 300ft in height. It was described by Sir Nikolaus Pevsner, the eminent art historian as 'the most prodigious romantic folly in England'. This extraordinary building was created at least partly to annoy and browbeat unfriendly and disapproving local landowners. It may have been a two-fingers gesture, but Beckford's private anguish is hinted at in his statement, 'Some people drink to forget their unhappiness. I do not drink. I build.' His loneliness was emphasised by the building of a wall seven miles long, 12ft high and topped by sharp spikes, around the estate. Loose bloodhounds roamed the demesne at night. They were fed in the morning.

Build he did. Work started in October 1796 but he was in such a hurry to complete it that corners were cut. The foundations were inadequate for a building of this size, the materials were too flimsy, his relationship with Wyatt largely a fraught and hostile one and, worst of all, Beckford plied his workers with copious quantities of beer which he mistakenly thought would spur them on to greater efforts. In reality they were frequently working in such a state of alcoholic befuddlement that they wouldn't have known their architraves from their aedicules. Fonthill Abbey took six years to build, but only a few moments to collapse. No sooner had the dust descended on the tortured pile of broken masonry which was to have been his home than he resolved to rebuild Fonthill Abbey. Again corners were cut and the building was approaching completion when an ominous but familiar rumble was followed by an ear-shattering crash as large parts of the fabric collapsed once more.

They say that eccentrics are natural optimists, at least so far as their obsessions are concerned. However the works at Fonthill had been so expensive that even Beckford realised that he couldn't afford a second rebuilding. Fonthill was put on the market and with the money he obtained from the auction, he bought himself two adjacent houses in Lansdown Crescent in Bath, which he then somewhat eccentrically joined with a little flying footbridge for use when he moved from one to the other. This quirky constructional feature can still be seen. The glory days of Bath were over and it is likely that Beckford felt reasonably comfortable living in what by his standards were somewhat straitened circumstances in a city which was still genteel but certainly a little down-at-heel and where there were now few, if any, of that particular breed of his social superiors who were likely to enjoy trying to snub and patronise him.

Beckford still had sufficient means to buy up an area of land on Lansdown a mile or more away from his residences and this enabled him to reprise his obsession with vertical construction. It is said that he acquired a stretch of garden which was very narrow but extended all the way from Lansdown Crescent to this site. Whether he had learned that attempts to imitate the Tower of Babel were bound to end in failure or that funds were relatively limited, this tower,

Beckford's grave and tower

Angel in Lansdown Cemetery

Gatehouse to Lansdown Cemetery

though still very impressive, was a mere 130 or 154ft high, depending on which account you read. It is more likely to be the latter. It was designed and the construction supervised by a friend of Beckford's by the name of Goodridge. It was completed in 1827. Happily it was built sufficiently well to continue standing proudly to this day. Beckford described the tower as his 'sepulchre' and stuffed it with those items from his vast and magnificent collection of antiquities, objets d'art and books that he simply had been unable to part with so that the tower was in effect was his third home.

Beckford's Tower has been superbly renovated in recent years and as well as containing residential accommodation let by the Landmark Trust, there is an excellent small museum which contains a wealth of material relating to Beckford. From the top of the tower on a clear day the distant mountains in Wales north of Abergavenny may be seen, as well as the Downs around Marlborough, the Cotswolds and the Mendips. Beckford proudly described the view from the top of the tower as 'the finest prospect in Europe'. The tower has a kind of lantern top and when this is illuminated, the effect is quite stunning.

Goodridge and Beckford himself are buried in the cemetery adjoining the tower. It is only to be expected that in the case of such an extraordinary man, there are stories that his spirit continues to hang around the place where his mortal remains lie. He is still grumpy, so it is said, which is why he is thought to take great exception to certain of those who visit his grave. To show his displeasure, he knocks them off their feet! Absurd although it may seem, in our present health and safety-conscious world when it is dinned into us that accidents, those that are serious but also some that are absolutely trivial, must be reported, there have indeed been a small but significant number of people who have gone on record as having taken a spill for no very obvious reason while in the neighbourhood of Beckford's grave.

Even if Beckford only occasionally stayed overnight in his tower, he either walked briskly or rode every day to and from Lansdown Crescent. He frequently galloped over the downs. He remained hale and hearty well into old age and over the years witnesses claim to have seen a spectral figure accompanied by a dog either walking or riding the well-worn route between his town houses and the tower. What is less well-known is that at first the burial of Beckford by his tower was refused because the ground was not consecrated and so he was interred in Bath Abbey instead. It was 1848 before the area close to the tower was licensed for burials and so Beckford's remains were brought up the hill from the abbey and laid to rest where his rather spectacular tomb can still be seen. As noted above, it is a moot point whether his spirit is actually taking the rest to which it is entitled. Superstitious people were always concerned when mortal remains were moved, even if it was done reverentially, and no sooner was Beckford in his grave at Landsown than the gossip-mongers got to work relating with gloomy relish how his ghost was at large roaming the area in the hours of darkness.

Beckford always got on better with animals than with humans. His favourite pet dog was buried close to the tower. At a later stage, its remains were disinterred and placed nearer those of Beckford. A number of reports have described the appearance of a spectral dog and the sound of disembodied barking in the area around the tower and the nearby cemetery.

It says something about the impression Beckford made in his lifetime that not only was his funeral the most spectacular ever seen in Bath, but that 20,000 people turned out to watch the funeral cortege make its way from Lansdown Crescent to the Abbey.

Larkhall Place

Larkhall Place is off St Saviour's Road in the north-east part of the city. Some years ago the owner was seriously spooked when on a number of occasions she saw what she described as a spectral nun in black with only a blur where her face should have been. The owner experienced no particular fear when the figure appeared although she found the musty smell that it seemed to exude somewhat repulsive. Sometimes she heard her name being called when the house was otherwise empty, and put this down to the presence of the faceless nun. If it had no face, how could it call out?

Footpath rear of Larkhall Place

Above: Laura Place

Left: Linley House, Pierrepoint Place

Laura Place

At the junction of Henrietta, Johnstone and Great Pulteney streets, and adorned with a working fountain which motorists probably resent, Laura Place is reputed to be haunted by the occasional sound of clattering harness and trotting horses and the sensation of displaced air as if a horse-drawn carriage or a stage coach is just passing.

Linley House, Pierrepont Place

Linley House was formerly the Bath Festival Office. In the 1950s a flat in the building was occupied by a woman who was often alarmed to hear footsteps when she knew there was no one on the premises to make such a noise. On occasions, one or more doors would open, apparently of their own accord but seemingly in conjunction with the disembodied footsteps. These phenomena had been going on for some time and were taking their toll, so the tenant asked a male friend to come and stay and give her some moral support. Before long, the by now familiar footsteps obliged and could be heard approaching the door. Her friend leaped up and flung the door open. There was nothing to be seen!

Perhaps the presence of a man spooked whatever it was that produced the mysterious sound of footsteps because, after that time, they were heard no more.

Milsom Street

Milsom Street is a wide and elegant major shopping street right in the centre of Bath. For many years, several shops have reported the apparent presence on their premises of a ghost or perhaps a poltergeist who is seemingly obsessed with saving electricity! This eco-warrior of the spirit world turns lights off apparently at random but often when the occupiers of the retail premises would actually prefer them to be on, for example to illuminate and display their wares to passers-by during the hours of darkness, or for reasons of security. This elusive presence does not just restrict itself to turning off shop window displays but sometimes turns lights off in other parts of the building, even at times when there are members of staff on the premises. It also has a penchant for closing doors and turning televisions on and off.

This phenomenon is reckoned to be the ghost of a former occupant of the premises who was regarded locally as something of a crank because of his obsession with turning lights off and closing doors.

Northgate Street

This is a short and very busy street on the east side of the city centre. One of the premises in this street was occupied by an old-established firm of bridal outfitters. In 1978 the company was displaying in its window a costume which had been made on the premises to the orders of a local dramatic society. The dress drew some admiring glances from passers-by but its presence seemed to rouse the well-known and long-standing ghost of Northgate Street to previously undreamt-of heights of rage. This ghost was known to all and sundry as 'Miss Hunt' and its presence was accepted with considerable nonchalance over the years by those who worked in the shop, although it was generally reckoned to live next door.

'Miss Hunt' seems to have been a mild if slightly eccentric ghost who could be seen out of the corner of the eye flitting around the place minding her own business but vanishing as soon as anyone aware of her presence tried to get a better look at her. She was prone to wandering about the place when it was empty after hours and absent-mindedly turning on lights that should be off and, of course, vice versa. This habit, as well as that of opening doors that should be shut and closing those required to be left open, was regarded as little more than a peccadillo. This sort of thing had been going on for years but the arrival of the dress in the window clearly provoked wrath in the bosom of this normally very placid ghost.

The dress resembled the kind of thing that Mary, Queen of Scots would have worn and was indeed meant to resemble what a well-to-do woman of the Elizabethan period might have worn. Why this was anathema to 'Miss Hunt' we shall never know but it caused her to change the habits of a lifetime, if such a word can be applied to a ghost. She spent the first day that the dress went on show appearing, vanishing and then reappearing so frequently that she made the staff quite dizzy. Much worse however was the fact that she seems to have drawn on

An alley off Northgate Street

special effects to exude a singularly disgusting, dank, mouldy smell as she moved around the premises. This was all too much for the proprietor and the staff. They got their heads together and decided that the only possible cause for 'Miss Hunt's' deviation from the norm was the presence of the dress. The unanimous decision was taken to remove it from the shop window. Next day the staff waited with bated breath, being greatly relieved when there were no further appearances by 'Miss Hunt'. Better than that, there was no repetition of the repulsive smell she seemed to be responsible for. They were happy and presumably the ghost was happy too.

It is generally thought that 'Miss Hunt' was the ghost of a woman who had committed suicide in the building next door which was generally thought to be her 'base'.

Old King Street

Old King Street is a very short street in the city centre. In the mid-1980s a building in the street came to make the news because of the sudden and unexpected manifestation of ghostly noises where none had apparently ever been experienced before. The lives of those occupying the premises were made miserable by what was believed to be the ghosts of two young men who insisted on stamping around loudly on the floors of upstairs rooms. They also constantly rattled door knobs and handles and succeeded in making a noise like that of smashing crockery, a sound that is fairly unmistakeable. These noises became so troublesome that one of the occupiers mentioned the problem to a number of people and as a result a séance was organised. During the séance a medium claimed to have got in touch with the spirits of the two young men and explained patiently but firmly that what they were doing was inconsiderate and was making life unpleasant for the human denizens. After all they paid rent to live there and the tenancy agreement said nothing about having to live with ghostly sounds. The holding of séances and the work of mediums both provoke scepticism in many quarters but it seems as if these two ghosts were the epitome of reasonableness because the noises ceased immediately and have never returned.

As a footnote, the events in Old King Street provoked considerable interest in psychic circles and investigators claim to have identified the spirits as being, respectively, those of a young man who died on a motor-cycle in a road traffic accident and a youth who suffered from chronic asthma and had one final attack which proved to be fatal.

Park Street

Park Street stands a short distance from the centre of Bath close to the open space known as High Common. Early in the 1990s two girls sharing a flat in this street reported a number of occasions on which footsteps were heard running up the stairs to be followed by an outburst of insistent rapping on the door to the flat. This phenomenon was widely reported in the local newspapers and correspondence ensued in which a number of people wrote of the house being haunted for a century or more by the ghost of a man who had spent much of his married life systematically beating his wife and inflicting frightful injuries on her. In his latter years, he became afraid that when he died he might be called upon to atone for his behaviour, although his anxieties in this respect did not inhibit him from continuing the assaults on his wife. His punishment seems to have been that his soul was not allowed to find repose and is forced, every so often, to return to the scene of his cruel acts where he remains in the state of restlessness and apprehension in which he had been when he died.

Old King
Street

Popjoy's Restaurant, Saw Close, now Strada

Beau Nash once lived in this building, right in the centre of the city next to the Theatre Royal and now a restaurant with a fine reputation for its cuisine. Nash had a liking for the company of women and he is said to have enjoyed many, and varied, relationships with them. His last mistress is supposed to have been a Juliana Popjoy who lived with him in this town house. Is it Juliana who has appeared from time to time upstairs in a room used by diners for aperitifs before they sat down to their meals? At least one would-be diner rushed out of the building and refused to come back when he had been sitting alone sipping a pre-dinner drink only to find a lady dressed in eighteenth-century clothing sitting next to him who then promptly vanished! It is known that Juliana was exceptionally distraught at Nash's death, so perhaps she never left the scene of their happy cohabitation.

She may not be alone. A female figure has occasionally been seen apparently dining alone but there is no point in attempting to serve her because, when approached, she also vanishes. Credibility is stretched when stories have circulated that Juliana as a ghost can turn from a lovely young woman into a repulsive hag and back again at will.

No.71 Pulteney Street

Great Pulteney Street runs impressively, if a trifle monotonously, dead straight from Laura Place to Sydney Place on the eastern side of the city. It was intended to be part of a much larger development which foundered because of the financial crisis of 1793.

Strada, formerly Popjoys

The Beau Nash plaque on Strada

No.71 Pulteney Street

No.71 is haunted by the ghost of none other than one of England's most distinguished old sea dogs. This was Richard Howe (1726-99) who became the first Earl Howe and First Lord of the Admiralty towards the end of a glittering naval career where he gained the reputation of being somewhat taciturn but very fair-minded so far as the grievances of the men under his command were concerned, he was very popular. He spent his declining years at Bath. He has been seen on a number of occasions pacing, much as he might have done on his own quarterdeck, and in his full regalia as if engaged in an inspection. Sometimes he has been heard rather than seen, the noises sounding for all the world as if he has come in after having been out in a storm and he is perhaps wearing a tarpaulin cape which he is shaking to get rid of the drops. Solid walls are no impediment to this ghost's movements and it seems as if he occasionally pops next door for a look around.

Queen Square

The house in Queen Square once occupied by John Wood the Elder is said to be haunted by the ghost of a woman known as Sylvia, but whose real name was Frances Braddock. She was the daughter of the famous soldier Edward Braddock who died in an ambush in 1755 when commanding British troops on their way to lay siege to Fort Dusquene, later known as Pittsburgh, during the wars against the French and the Native Americans.

Sylvia, the name by which we will call her here, was a compulsive gambler who managed to work her way through an inheritance worth hundreds of thousands of pounds by today's standards. She added to her woes by being duped by a succession of rapacious conmen who enjoyed her sexual favours and promised her their everlasting love while simultaneously winkling out of her what was left of her fortune and then disappearing over the horizon.

She was an attractive young woman but was down on her uppers by the time she moved into John Wood's house. One of the most endearing aspects of the history of Bath is the way that it has managed to combine architectural charm and the superficial respectability accompanying expensive taste on the one hand, with raffishness and disregard for accepted social norms on the other. This was an unorthodox arrangement whereby a young, unmarried woman went to reside in the house of one of Bath's most prominent citizens, ostensibly to be on hand to help with various household tasks but in fact to live as a member of the family, enjoying the quality of life Wood's status brought with it. She moved in with the Wood ménage and it is clear that part of the arrangement was that she slept with Wood when the opportunity arose.

On the face of it, this would seem to have been a pretty satisfactory *modus vivendi*, at least for Wood and Sylvia. Although no-one in fashionable Bath society actually uttered any criticisms that were heard by Sylvia, she felt the insidious pressure of unspoken disapproval and took it to heart. Wood's status was such that he received in his house the most glittering of Bath's ultra-fashionable residents and visitors. Sylvia was refined and personable and used to mixing in such circles but those who visited, despite being charmed by her, began to comment that she seemed increasingly ill-at-ease and melancholic. It did not help that she had huge undischarged gambling debts.

Evidently she felt so guilty about her situation that she resolved to do away with herself. It is known that she visited a local doctor and quizzed him on how best to commit suicide and indeed that she made a couple of unsuccessful attempts to achieve that objective. Wood's business interests often took him away from home for several days at a time and he was frequently accompanied by his family. It was on one of these occasions that Sylvia succeeded in launching herself into eternity. Rather melodramatically, she dressed herself in a white robe, perhaps suggestive of virginity, or at least a wry witness to the loss of that rare but exalted state, placed a noose of strong silk around her neck, kicked away the stool on which she was standing but the noose broke and she fell to the floor with a resounding bump. Second time round she gained her objective, dying quickly but in extreme agony because her tongue was bitten through several times. Before that, she had apparently scratched some kind of message in verse on a window with her ring. It was to the effect that she saw death as a blessed release from all her problems.

The inquest recorded a verdict of death by her own hand because she was the victim of 'lunacy'. Nowadays it would probably be said rather more euphemistically or perhaps just kindly that she died 'severely traumatised'. She was buried in the Braddock family vault in the Abbey in September 1731. Wood was apparently heartbroken when he heard of her death and those who knew him strongly asserted that he was never the same man again. Who are we say to say whether this response was out of frustrated sexual desire or the result of genuine love for the poor girl?

The Royal Crescent

Nos 8-10 Queen Street

This narrow street stands close to Queen Square in central Bath. This building has produced reports of the sound of footsteps coming from an old wooden staircase, long since taken out of use and its entrance boarded up and plastered over. It is an old building dating back to about 1730 and on occasions the ghostly figure of a man dressed in old-fashioned attire, including a top hat, has been seen in the gentleman's toilets. In the 1980s the building was used as a restaurant.

Royal Crescent

This world-famous architectural tour de force (at least at the front) has apparently witnessed the drawing up and subsequent departure of an elegant coach, drawn by four dapple grey horses. This cameo is apparently the re-enactment of the elopement from No. 11 of the young lady of the house with the eminent Irish playwright Richard Brinsley Sheridan (1751-1816) in 1773. The young lady was Elizabeth Linley but although Sheridan went on to considerable success with the plays he wrote and his theatrical enterprises, as well as making a name for himself as an orator when he entered Parliament, the latter years of his career were plagued with bad luck and he lived in poverty. The marriage was not a great success because Sheridan was a serial philanderer.

Royal Mineral Water Hospital

Can we call this a ghost (deceased)? This building which was erected in the eighteenth century as a charitable gesture to provide facilities for the genuinely poor who visited Bath for therapy is of course no longer used as a hospital. The ghostly phenomena associated with it have not manifested themselves for the best part of fifty years. A nurse is known to have committed suicide on the premises and there have been sightings of an old-fashioned figure in grey and wearing a nurse's uniform. In the past there were many reports of what sounded like a woman's footsteps, teetering along in high heels, advancing, passing and then retreating into the distance. Was this the ghost of a visitor, since you would not expect a nurse on duty to be shod in that kind of footwear?

St James's Burial Ground

Opposite the Lamb & Lion pub in Lower Borough Walls in the city centre stands St James Burial Ground, which locals refer to as 'Pigeon Park'. The former church of St James has long since gone but the churchyard remains consecrated ground. It is possible that in the Middle Ages witches were burned at the stake at this point. Local legend says that this central and commercially valuable spot has not been developed because back in the fifteenth century the last expiring words of a witch who was being consumed by the flames were a curse on the soil on which the stake was placed. In reality it seems unlikely that the forces of big business would allow such considerations to stand in the way of building development. It is the kind of place that might be haunted given its bloody past but the author has not come across any such reports. Nor does it look haunted.

St John's Court

It does not do to take some alleged ghost stories too seriously. St John's Court is on the east side of the River Avon off St John's Road. There was a kerfuffle there in 1733 when the tenancy was taken by a Quaker gentleman of considerable means. His business often took him away from Bath and in his absence the housekeeper looked after things. It wasn't long before she started complaining that she could not sleep because of all sorts of untoward and menacing noises. These she thought were created by ghosts and she informed her master that she was leaving forthwith. He could not brook the idea of ghosts and so he wished her well and let her go. Rumours were already circulating about ghosts in St John's Court and these were intolerable for a man as

Left: The Royal Mineral Water hospital

Below: St James's Burial Ground

rationalist on such matters as he was. He and his wife decided to move into the housekeeper's bedroom for just as long as it took to scotch these absurd notions. This proved to be a mistake. The couple spent two terrifying nights listening to the spooky sounds and found the whole thing so frightening that, as one of their neighbours put it delicately, they soiled the bed linen.

Our Quaker now began to question notions he had long held dear about the existence or non-existence of supernatural phenomena. The whole neighbourhood was buzzing with rumours about the ghost or ghosts and ever more far-fetched stories began circulating about murders that had taken place on the premises and bodies that had been cut up and buried there. A large group of busy-bodies prevailed on the owner to let them stay overnight in the haunted room. Nothing of significance was heard until a flaming row broke out between the owner and some of his sillier guests. This became more acrimonious by the minute and lasted long enough for the spectators to forget all about the ghosts and thoroughly enjoy a great night's entertainment listening to the invective being thrown hither and thither.

The issue of the haunting therefore remained unresolved until the owner decided to hire a tough navvy to stay in the room overnight. This man totally lacked the kind of imagination that would create a whole army of spectres and ghouls where none existed. He soon traced the noise to a casement window which, under certain conditions, moved backwards and forwards making a quite extraordinary racket through the otherwise silent house. Closing the window firmly put an end to the ghostly noises and shut the gossipers up.

This whole story has more than a hint of the apocryphal…

Salamander, John Street

John Street is right in the city centre and this building, which was originally a coffee house dating from the eighteenth century, only recently became a pub. Patrons could easily be mistaken for believing that it has been a pub for centuries, such is its historic feeling and atmosphere. In the time it has been a pub, it has gained a reputation for being haunted. Reported phenomena have been occasional glasses seemingly thrown by invisible hands, a particular spot which exudes an unpleasant chill and footsteps resounding upstairs when the only living people on the premises were downstairs.

Saville Row, Bennett Street, Russell Street

These are all close to The Circus and to the Assembly Rooms and together provide the location for one of Bath's best-known ghostly manifestations. This is 'The Man in the Black Hat', or more simply 'The Man in Black'. He has been seen by so many witnesses that it is possible to build up a composite picture, especially since some of them took the trouble to sketch what they saw for the record. His hat is large, black and has a rim. He wears a black coat, three-quarters length and generously cut, possibly breeches and gaiters, longish hair and has a distinctly old-fashioned look. At least one observer described him as an elderly man and bent or at least stooped. He has the power to vanish in an instant but he does not seem to inspire strong feelings of fear.

No explanation seems to have been put forward as to the reasons for his appearance or even, indeed, if he is a ghost, as to whose ghost he actually is. He has staying power. He was first reported in the 1800s.

Above left: Interior staircase, Salamander pub

Above right: Exterior of Salamander

Left: Alfred Street, near Saville Row

Sham Castle, Bathampton Down

Britain seems to have more than its fair share of ghostly associations. It also has very large numbers of what are loosely called 'follies'. We should be very pleased on both counts. Oddities and curiosities are one of the delights of town and countryside in the United Kingdom. While it may be true that follies are buildings which exhibit the folly of those who built them, it is not true to say that follies are simply useless structures without a purpose. A mock ruin; a prospect tower; an eye-catcher; an obelisk: all of these have a purpose if only to be seen and to give pleasure to those who created them. That should be enough.

Bath might be expected to have one or two follies and it does not disappoint in this respect. The 'Sham Castle' stands high above the city on Bathwick Hill. This quirky little erection was the work of Ralph Allen (1694-1764) who with John Wood the Elder and John Wood the Younger contributed much to making Bath the place that rightly regarded itself as the second city of England while it was enjoying the height of its success as a spa town in the eighteenth century. Allen made his wealth by securing the position of Post Master and reorganising the local postal services, as well as owning the quarries from which the stone was extracted to build

Ralph Allen's Sham Castle – what horrors are seen at night through the arch?

Ralph Allen's Sham Castle

the fronts of the marvellously elegant Georgian houses, crescents and terraces which people come from right across the world to see. While Allen was merely accumulating a fortune as opposed to eventually becoming a multi-millionaire by today's standards, he built a house in the city centre in Old Lilliput Alley and decided it would give him pleasure and add to his kudos if he had an eye-catcher built on an eminence where it could be seen by himself and by other Bath citizens. The result is a charming little folly, perhaps best seen from a distance where its *trompe l'oeil* effect is not so obvious. This is because at close quarters it reveals itself to be exactly what it is; that is, a façade, pure and simple. It was built in 1762 and displays many features of real castles. All the effort was put into its frontage and to look around the back is to experience a real sense of anti-climax. It is floodlit at night and is clearly visible from the city centre. At one time it was white-washed and would have been even more eye-catching. Claims have been made that Ralph Allen's ghost has been seen at the site from time to time, apparently returning in order to see that everything is ship-shape and Bristol fashion with the strange little building of which he was apparently enormously proud.

A more sinister phenomenon has been seen on several occasions close by on Bathampton Down and, perhaps fortunately, only at night. It has been described, not very precisely, as a 'large luminous shape' apparently slithering along the top of a stone wall close-by. Away from street lighting, visibility is often quite good even on nights without a moon. This 'thing' has been seen by a number of those who choose to walk in the vicinity during the hours of darkness, these being mainly but not exclusively people walking their dogs. One such walker described what happened. Whatever it was, the dogs saw or sensed it before he did. The effect on the dogs was instantaneous.

They stopped, their hackles rose and showing every sign of being seriously frightened, they started barking although the walker described the noise they made as rather more like a hysterical yowl. He then described a vague shape – definitely not human – moving along the top of the wall. It was only visible for a split second before vanishing from sight. Whatever it was had evidently gone because the dogs' immediate response was to relax and then to tug on their leads as if they were eager to get on with the walk. What is it that slithers so menacingly along the top of that stone wall?

Star Inn, Vineyards

On the A4 just north of the city centre, this is one of Bath's most characterful pubs, a must for the author whenever he is town. The Star is as town pubs once used to be – basic but friendly, welcoming and a real centre of the community serving all ages and classes. Its layout and fittings with several distinct areas and wood panelling would drive today's generation of pub interior designers to distraction but they are all the better for that. The pub has scarcely changed in decades and needs no plasma televisions, no flashing fruit machines waiting greedily to gulp the money of the hopeful but gullible and no 'gastro-food' to please its discriminating clientele.

It is often described as having a coffin-like appearance as it is approached from the city centre and it is haunted, on occasions, by a mischievous spirit called 'Pickford' whose main activity seems to be to cause smallish objects to fall off the wall and onto selected members of the pub's regular customers, much to the amusement of the others. One particular, somewhat unyielding, wooden bench used by the regulars is called 'Death Row'.

Interior of Star Inn

Bar area of Star Inn   Exterior of Star Inn, Vineyards

Swallow Street

This short street in the city centre contains the Old Boiler House where the ghost of a young woman has been seen. The sad figure is said to be the victim of a murder in that building.

Sydney Place

Sydney Place is approached from the city centre via Great Pulteney Street and fronts the Holburne Museum of Art. The large houses along parts of Sydney Place are mostly divided into apartments and one of these has witnessed unexplained happenings for many years. They have centred on one of the bedrooms and have included insistent rappings on the door, apparent nocturnal attempts to remove the bedclothes and the rather indistinct appearance of a male figure. This figure has been seen on a number of occasions, once apparently carrying bagpipes which, thankfully, he was not playing or the neighbours might have had something to say. Another apparition has been glimpsed on the stairs and this may account for the sound of footsteps on occasions when there was no one alive to make them.

Left: The Old Boiler House

Opposite: Holbourne Museum, Sydney Place

Theatre Royal, Saw Close

The Theatre Royal, Bath, is one of Britain's best-loved playhouses. The first theatre in the city was opened around 1705 and stood on the site of what became the well-known Royal Mineral Water Hospital. That a town as small as Bath at that time had its own theatre was an indication that the place was being sought out by the wealthy and fashionable elements of society who wanted amenities of a superior sort. A second theatre was built in Orchard Street which was replaced in 1805 by the present building. By the late 1760s it had been granted a Royal Charter and was regarded as the most important theatre outside London. Among the early celebrities to tread the boards there was Sarah Siddons (1755-1831), she of the immensely expressive and near-beautiful face, superb figure, regal bearing and infinitely rich voice. The Theatre Royal enjoyed a century or more of great success but had began to fall into the doldrums before it suffered a destructive fire in 1862. The decision was taken to rebuild it and as so often happened in those days where a prestigious contract was on offer, a competition was held inviting architects to submit designs. It was won by a local man, C. J. Phipps, who went on to become the country's leading theatre designer.

The ghosts of the Theatre Royal and those of the Garrick's Head next door are intertwined, as indeed are the histories and even parts of the fabric of the two buildings. We have already mentioned in the section about the Garrick's Head the young woman who committed suicide by leaping from a window when her husband had killed her supposed lover with a sword. One version of this story says that she was an actress at the theatre. The suicide was either from an upper window in the theatre or from the pub depending on which account is referred to. The story goes that the girl was exceptionally attractive and that the man became entranced by her looks and, presumably, her thespian qualities. Apparently he went to every performance in which she had a part, always sat by himself in the same box and spent the whole time gazing soulfully at his heart's delight. Whether or not this adoration from afar eventually developed into a sexual liaison we shall never know, but the version that says that she jumped from an upper floor of the theatre also states that she did so wearing the long grey dress and the feathers in her hair with which she was adorned while acting her part. Be that as it may, naturally her ghost when it has revisited the theatre and the pub has become known as the 'Grey Lady'. She has the unusual and rather disconcerting ability to pass diagonally through rows of seats, thankfully when they are empty. She does not stay around for long but she is said always to be wearing white lace gloves.

A pub can often attract a little extra business if it makes it known that as well as serving spirits it provides accommodation for them! The lady in grey does appear in the Garrick's Head on occasions but seems to be fonder of the theatre, although even there she has proved somewhat elusive. Back in 1920 the eminent Russian ballerina Anna Pavlova, who knew nothing about the story, asked casually about the very old-fashioned looking woman in grey sitting alone in one of the boxes. She was somewhat dumfounded when the staff in the box office told her that the particular box she had indicated had remained unsold and therefore empty during that performance. Members of staff, however, were less surprised – they had heard it all before. Dame Anna Neagle (1904-1986), a very fine actress, was known for her very down-to-earth and matter-of-fact attitude to life. But she admitted to having seen in one of the boxes, otherwise empty, a rather diaphanous figure apparently dressed in an old-fashioned grey dress who was also wearing one of those extraordinary and rather silly creations, fashionable in times long ago, a hat profusely covered in feathers.

A very curious legend of the supernatural kind has grown up around the theatre. It concerns the expected annual appearance of a peacock butterfly which supposedly brings good luck with it. The Theatre Royal was run by the Maddox family between 1926 and 1976. They were immensely proud of the theatre and determined to keep it both enterprising and innovative. They revived the staging of family pantomimes and these are still regarded as being among the very best in the country. In 1938, Reg Maddox, the senior member of the family, decided that the production that year should be *Aladdin*. It was to have a gorgeous butterfly theme with the dancers dressed appropriately. The backdrop was to consist of a giant peacock butterfly. The peacock butterfly (*Nymphalis io*) is a large, handsome butterfly with four conspicuous eye-spots which resemble the markings on a peacock's tail. It passes the winter in the butterfly stage, sleeping in a hollow tree or some convenient interstice in a building or elsewhere.

At one of the rehearsals those involved were surprised when a peacock butterfly appeared, fluttering about as such creatures do and then landing on the stage. Something had perhaps dislodged it from its cosy hibernation spot up high up in the rafters but it seemed something of a coincidence given the decorative theme being employed for the pantomime. A few hours later, Reg Maddox had a heart attack. He died soon afterwards. This event obviously blighted the production and it was decided to remove the butterfly theme on the grounds that it might be an ill omen. The following year Reg's son, Frank Maddox, took over production of the pantomime which was to be *Aladdin* once more. Understandably, it was decided to dispense with the butterfly theme when what should happen but another peacock butterfly appeared on the stage. What's more, it landed in exactly the same spot as its predecessor the previous year. This was an extraordinary coincidence and Reg, having decided that it was a good omen after all, immediately resolved to restore the butterfly theme. *Aladdin* had an exceptionally successful season.

The tradition developed that a live peacock butterfly had to appear every winter before the season started in order to guarantee that the pantomime would be successful. In 1979 the opening performance of *Aladdin* featured the well-known stage figure of Leslie Crowther, playing the character 'Wishy Washy'. He was aware of the superstition concerning the butterfly and being of a somewhat superstitious nature, was more than a little concerned that the butterfly had not yet appeared. A thorough professional, he did not let his concerns show as he was breaking the ice with the audience when, as if the whole thing was stage-managed, the spotlight homed in on a peacock butterfly fluttering downwards and landing, to a great burst of applause, on the lapel of a slightly bemused but greatly relieved Crowther. Now he knew for sure that the show was going to be a great success. It became an even greater one when the butterfly, in the apparently random manner of its kind, took wing again only to flutter, land, flutter and land again with apparent fascination around the flies of Crowther's trousers. This brought the house down, as they say, but Crowther, aware that the show was tightly timed, scooped the butterfly up and then released it, whereupon its part in the day's activities was over. It was last seen heading for the wings, very appropriate for a butterfly.

A peacock butterfly (was it the same one?) appeared several more times while *Aladdin* was showing during what proved to be a particularly successful season. Since then a number of other celebrities claim to have seen the butterfly. They include Honor Blackman. She was perhaps best-known for her role as the ambiguously-named 'Pussy Galore' in the James Bond movie *Goldfinger*. However on this occasion she was earning an honest penny as the wicked fairy in another pantomime, *Jack and the Beanstalk,* and she too witnessed a butterfly well out of its season, fluttering about the stage area of the theatre like a good luck charm.

A cynic would say that theatres attract ghostly and supernatural stories because their whole *raison d'etre,* as well as that of the people who work in them, is concerned with make-belief. The author is only a humble historian who cannot possibly comment on that viewpoint but it is interesting to note that about thirty years ago, there was a mini-crisis in the theatre when one of the actors failed to turn up. A search of his dressing room produced no clues as to his whereabouts but did reveal a dead peacock butterfly. Later that night, the police broke into his lodgings and found him. He was dead. He had hanged himself.

There are those who say that the butterfly 'thing' is simply a stunt invented by the management to put bums on seats at what would otherwise be slack times. Certainly the management tried to get children involved by inviting them up onto the stage and organising a competition to see who could be the first to spot a butterfly. In the less materialistic days of the 1950s, the winner probably had a prize of an apple or a mandarin orange. It is difficult to envisage today's young captive consumers putting themselves out for such a prize. However the butterfly of the Theatre Royal is a fine example of the creation of a new legend.

After the exotic tales of the butterfly, all else dealing with supernatural aspects of the Theatre Royal might seem a trifle mundane but a host of other phenomena have been reported. An old lady has purportedly been seen, apparently skulking in the shadows and described as either nodding vigorously or rocking to and fro. Once the viewer catches sight of her, she gradually fades away. Occasionally she can be seen clearly but more often her figure is wispy and indistinct. More dramatic have been the occasional reports of a poltergeist. On one occasion a barman claimed that he had been hit by a full bottle of spirits aimed at him by an invisible assailant. It is not known how much damage was done to him or indeed to the bottle and, more importantly, to its contents. A malevolent poltergeist was blamed. One evening a woman was making her way up the stairs to the dress circle when a friend she knew well came running, almost falling, down the stairs and rushed past, seemingly oblivious of her presence. She was a little put out by the lack of acknowledgement and also the harassed look on her friend's face. She was a great deal more put out to learn when she got home that this friend had in fact died a few days earlier!

In June 1963 a new play was having its premiere at the Theatre Royal during that year's Bath Festival. A clock being used as a prop suddenly chimed and struck the hour during the performance. No logical explanation could be offered for how this could have happened given that the clock had had its mechanism removed precisely to prevent such an occurrence. The arms on the dial showed the time as half-past twelve but the clock struck three! No sooner had the chiming stopped than the house lights momentarily dimmed three times. The unanimous opinion of the old hands among the backstage staff was that this was one of the theatre's ghosts at work.

The Theatre Royal and the Garrick's Head next door share a number of unexplained, perhaps supernatural phenomena. Doors and windows open and close seemingly of their own volition, objects are inexplicably moved around or hidden, only to reappear equally mysteriously and often in the most ridiculous places, footsteps are heard apparently ascending and descending non-existent staircases and there are the sounds of items being moved about in equally non-existent rooms. Staff have frequently described the creepy sense of being watched by unseen eyes. For some reason the eyes, though invisible, are thought to belong to a female.

In 1981 a group of fifteen local further education students staged a sponsored overnight ghost watch in the theatre. They kept a close lookout and wrote down anything untoward. Sadly, perhaps, the only untoward event of the night was a single scary scream. More positively, plenty of money was raised for good causes.

Bath Tramways Sports and Social Club, York Place, London Road

In 1985, a number of reports appeared in the local press concerning this working-men's club, perhaps not the kind of venue popularly associated with supernatural activity. These were to the effect that mysterious footsteps were being heard, doors and windows were both opening and closing of their own accord, and a rather grandiose chandelier had shown a marked propensity to swing to and fro without any apparent draught or other agency. These phenomena did not apparently last for long nor, as far as the author knows, have they been repeated since.

It is at best a partial explanation to reveal that the club was supposedly built on the site of a dwelling in which, during the nineteenth century, two young children were wilfully neglected, eventually dying of starvation. If this was the work of their restless spirits, why did they make their presence felt for such a short period?

Plaque for Bath Burial Ground

Upper Borough Walls

Upper Borough Walls is the curious name of a street right in the centre of Bath. One of the very few city-centre fish and chip shops can be found there and adjacent to this useful facility is a fragment of the old stone walls which formerly surrounded the city. At this point, the walls have a somewhat sinister reputation and have sometimes been described as 'The Groaning Wall'. A little courtyard down a step from the street allows the visitor to examine the wall at close quarters and at this point on innumerable occasions down the years sounds described as 'groaning' and 'wailing' have been heard. Oddly, although by no means uniquely in paranormal situations, these sounds only seem to be audible to certain people. Those who do hear them invite ridicule when they tell their companions to listen to the noises only of course to be told, firmly but a trifle mockingly, that there aren't any noises. Investigators, fascinated by these reports, have found no useful evidence either proving or disproving the existence of these phenomena.

In the courtyard a plaque can be seen which records the deaths of 238 people who died in the Bath General Hospital between 1736 and 1849 and whose remains were interred at this spot.

Victoria Park

The Royal Victoria Park stands a short distance to the north-west of the centre of Bath and is one of the great glories of the city. Over the years there have been claims of curious emanations

Left: Memorial to the Queen Victoria, Victoria Park

Below: A dozy looking lion on the memorial

from a particular tree in the park, these being described by some as a 'psychic breeze'. This theory avers that the air in its neighbourhood is somehow drawn to the tree because of highly charged emotions released at the scene in the past. It is known that Victoria Park was a favourite location for duels in the eighteenth century. Duelling was a particularly fatuous example of upper-class behaviour and the duels often led to the death of one, sometimes of both, contestants. It is said that one particular tree, that supposedly causing the 'psychic breeze', was often used as a place under which, or even against which, to place the bodies of the deceased while arrangements were made to obtain an undertaker. Are the extreme emotions released by a duel to the death still capable of making themselves felt, even if only to certain receptive people?

Widcombe Crescent

Widcombe Crescent is just off the bottom end of Widcombe Hill to the south-east of Bath city centre. In the late nineteenth century, No.1 was occupied by a comfortably-off and apparently conventional family. It consisted of the father who worked in what are now euphemistically known as 'financial services', his wife and their two sons. One day the man was called away to London to deal with some urgent business on behalf of his employer and he took his elder son with him. The mother and younger son stayed behind.

No sooner had he reached London than he received an urgent message to return home immediately. He was not given any reason for this peremptory summons but clearly the message was not the sort anyone wants to get so unexpectedly. It was therefore with a definite sense of trepidation and foreboding that he headed back to Bath post-haste. When he arrived home it was to be told that his wife had committed suicide by poisoning herself and that before doing so she had also attempted to murder the younger boy with poison. Somehow and against all the odds, the boy clung to life. It was only in the months to come that it became evident that the effect of the poison had been to stunt the boy's physical growth and he was to remain vertically challenged and affected mentally for the rest of his life.

Poor man! He and both his sons were obviously traumatised by this horrible experience. They all displayed considerable fortitude in attempting to come to terms with the tragedy, at least as far as it was possible to do so. They were having some success in their attempts to find a new *modus vivendi* as a family in this house of horrible memories when some while later the father's attempts to create a new normality were rudely interrupted by the appearance of a ghost on the stairs. This ghost only added to the unpleasantness of living in a house associated with tragedy. It was female and it bore an expression of sheer unrelieved malice which terrified the man of the house, the boys and the servants. The house only possessed one staircase but everyone went up and down it as rarely as possible and only then at top speed. It proved too much for the family and they moved away. A procession of new tenants moved in and equally quickly moved out. None of them were able to cope with encountering the presence on the stairs and what should have been a 'des res' proved increasingly difficult to let (this, of course, was in the days before mortgages were readily available) and the house's evil reputation went before it, doubtless picking up extra details, real or imagined as it went.

In due course the local parish priest took on the tenancy with his family. He was only too aware of the house's sinister reputation but perhaps he felt that the spirituality he would bring to the place as a man of the cloth might disconcert the evil presence, whatever it was, and persuade it to take itself off elsewhere. He was quickly disabused on this score. The ghost seemed to take singular exception to his presence and far from retreating it began to make its feelings clear by manifesting itself in every room in the house, rather than just on the stairs. The children were turning into nervous wrecks and the servants quit after just a few days while word got around and it proved increasingly difficult to recruit replacements. It was not that the evil-looking ghost was seen all the time. Far from it – its actual appearances were sporadic and unpredictable but for all that it managed to cast a pall of fear over the unhappy house.

Apparently incensed by the continued presence of the priest in what the ghost clearly regarded as its fiefdom, it stepped up the frequency of its visible manifestations. The ghost was clearly not in a mood to be reasoned with and the priest determined on an exorcism. This took place with no fewer than forty priests in attendance which could be regarded as a trifle heavy-handed. Perhaps the ghost thought so too because several of those attending the exorcism claimed to have seen it lurking in the doorway while the ritual was taking place.

Exorcism is a practice which has reduced considerably in the twentieth century. The concept that a place or a person can be 'possessed' by a ghost or an evil spirit dates back to the distant times of mankind but has become less prevalent with the decline of religious forms of

Widcombe
Crescent

superstition and a greater understanding of the workings of the human mind. In many cases those earlier generations would have thought of as being 'possessed' are now thought to be suffering from a variety of mental illnesses. Whatever the viability of exorcism, it seems to have worked at No. 1 and the occupants were able to settle down to an existence unspoilt by the appearance of the savage-looking woman on the stairs or indeed anywhere else in the house. There have been no further reports of untoward events. Where did the ghost go?

Widcombe Crescent seems to be an unwontedly haunted part of the city. At No. 10 an old lady lived with one of her grown-up step-daughters and her family. She was good for her age but increasingly she preferred to spend her time in her bedroom which was directly above the dining room. On day she fell out of her chair, landing with a loud thump. This was not only heard by the rest of the family having Sunday lunch in the room below but it also set the glass chandeliers rattling with the vibration. The others rushed upstairs to find the old lady confused and somewhat shaken but largely unhurt. However she was clearly affected by the fall and went into decline, dying some months later. After she had died, the family continued much as before except that they noticed that when they were having their Sunday get-together, which was always at the same time, they began to hear a thump uncannily like that which had indicated the fall of the old lady. On the first two or three occasions this happened, everyone rushed upstairs but of course nothing untoward was to be seen. In the weeks and months that followed, they simply heard the thump and continued with their meal. Was it the ghost of the old lady? If so, she went bump in the day rather than bump in the night.

Widcombe Terrace

Two sisters shared a house in Widcombe Terrace. The younger looked after the elder who was an invalid with serious mobility problems, largely confined to her bed. This arrangement had been going on for years. Naturally both sisters had got used to each other's company and had every reason to believe that they were the house's only occupants. It was therefore with both surprise and a little alarm that the younger sister, who was relaxing quietly at the end of the day, heard what she described as a severe bout of coughing coming from the passage beyond the closed door of the room in which she was sitting. She leapt up to see what was going on because the noise, although it sounded like that of a female, was certainly not her sister coughing. She did not give herself time to be really frightened and, flinging open the door, she was just about to call upstairs to her sister when, to her horror, her eyes took in the figure of an aged woman in old-fashioned clothes. Wearing a mob cap, this old woman looked for all the world like a domestic servant of the sort once employed in droves by the middle and upper classes. If the presence of this unexpected figure was not bad enough in itself, even more unnerving was her exceptionally lined and livid face, riven by a sinister, seemingly all-knowing leer. Things went from bad to worse. The woman wanted to call out but was too dumbstruck to do so. The apparition then waved an unpleasantly bony hand to and fro, one finger displaying an unexpectedly bright and shiny ring. She was somewhat mesmerised by the ring only to see the cadaverous hand turn into an equally cadaverous fist. With this the unwelcome guest gave a menacing gesture and then, having turned round, bounded up the stairs with extraordinary speed for one so seemingly frail, uttering a bloodcurdling cackle as she did so. The younger sister was clearly a woman of some fortitude because she

Widcombe Terrace

followed up the stairs, albeit more slowly, to make sure her sibling was safe and sound but also, doubtless, to pour out her story. Her sister was sound asleep – she had seen and heard nothing untoward.

Some weeks passed, the routine of the house returned to normal but of course the younger sister had not been able totally to expunge the horrid memories from her mind. The sisters' niece, a young woman of about twenty, came to stay with them for a few days. The two sisters agreed to say nothing about the earlier events, although in truth the older lady had a feeling that the whole episode was no more than an exceptionally vivid and horrifying dream experienced by her sister.

One evening the three occupants of the house had settled down for the night when the younger sister suddenly sat bolt upright in bed in her darkened bedroom. Something had apparently thumped against her door. Dreading a repetition of her previous experience, she hesitatingly opened the door. A light was on in the passage and she was confronted by a ghastly luminous figure of only semi-human appearance. It didn't help that this unwholesome 'thing' was naked and had a head the sister later described as 'dome-like'. The fact that it was slavering at the mouth and had piercing eyes only added to the horror.

The night's fearsome events were not over. Using every bit of pluck she could muster, she dashed past the loathsome spectre just as an appalling reverberating scream came from her niece's bedroom. She burst through the door, switching on the light to see the young woman sitting upright in her bed, shaking and clearly transported with terror. As if she couldn't bear to keep the experience to herself for a moment longer, she described how a noise had woken her whereupon she opened her eyes only to gaze into those of a hag-like creature glowing with a devilish luminosity. Her aunt did what she could to calm the near-hysterical young woman who was so frightened that they agreed that she would share her aunt's bed for the rest of the night. It is likely that sleep eluded the pair of them though not, apparently, the older sister who was amazed to hear about the night's goings-on when she woke in the morning. She had heard and seen nothing. The young woman left first thing, thanking them for their hospitality but doubtless swearing that she would never ever return to her aunts' wretched house.

Before the badly-shaken young lady left, she had swapped notes about her experience with that of her aunt. What the two had seen had obviously been the same apparition. She didn't know whether to be thankful or not that her aunts had omitted to mention the previous encounter with the cadaverous ghost flashing the shiny gold ring. Although the horrendous hag-like creature never reappeared, it was still capable of making its malevolent presence felt which meant that the two sisters got through an awful lot of domestic servants. These usually left, in some cases without even stopping to pick up their wages, claiming that certain parts of the house had such an awful threatening atmosphere that they entered them with their hearts in their mouths and their knees knocking. What was bad enough during the day was simply intolerable after dusk.

White Hart, Widcombe

In 1996 some of the locals were happily playing pool only to be transfixed and rooted to the spot when a figure came through the wall on one side of the room, passed through the pool

White Hart

No. 13 York Street

table and then disappeared through the wall on the opposite side to that which he had entered. This phenomenon which had never occurred before and has not occurred since, was witnessed by at least half-a-dozen customers, each of whom was prepared to testify that they saw what they said they saw.

No. 13 York Street

York Street runs alongside part of the Roman Baths in the city centre. These premises have three visible ghosts and one that is audible. The first is that of a boy who, while playing with a bouncy ball, somehow contrived to fall into a large container full of boiling water and died the agonising death that was the only possible outcome. His ghost is heard playing with a ball. The second ghost to manifest itself visibly is that of a street-walker who was lured into the house, assaulted and murdered. Next the corpse was dragged back onto the street and placed into a waiting coach which then rushed off pell-mell through the city to an unknown destination.

This scenario has supposedly been re-enacted on a number of occasions with a coachman who is apparently headless. Thirdly there is a ghost of a woman in white who hurries down a passage and passes through a closed door before disappearing.

Old alley leading to Eastgate and the river

The audible manifestation is the sound of the coach careering off over the cobbled streets of the city, whence no one knows.

It is not an explanation for these phenomena but it perhaps helps to know that this building stands on the site of the ancillary buildings attached to Bath Abbey and that building work has unearthed human bones, which suggest that the abbey's burial ground was in the vicinity.

FOUR

AROUND BATH

George, Bathampton

Bathampton is a pleasant village, surprisingly sequestered given its proximity to Bath. It is only about three miles east of the city off the A36 Warminster Road. In the churchyard lie many of the eighteenth and nineteenth-century bigwigs who made their homes in Bath and the surrounding district after distinguished careers in public life. They include Alexander Mackenzie, who attained the elevated rank of General in the Army, Roderick Murchison (1792-1871), an eminent geologist who predicted the discovery of gold in Australia and Admiral Arthur Phillip (1738-1814), who has already been mentioned in relation to hauntings in Bennett Street in the city centre. He was the first Governor of New South Wales. He had the reputation of being a humane and compassionate man, but that description sits paradoxically alongside his statement that the most incorrigible villains should be closely confined 'till an opportunity (is) offered of delivering them as prisoners to the natives of New Zealand and *let them eat them!*'

The pub is reputedly haunted by the ghost of a French aristocrat called Jean Baptiste de Barre. He was just the kind of man who the more radical elements in the French Revolution loved to seek out and then execute with the aid of the cunning device invented by the ingenious Dr Guillotine. Although this machine is indelibly associated with 'The Terror', it should be remembered that Guillotine was a gentle and kind man who deliberately designed his death machine to be a quick and efficient means of execution, providing the minimum of fuss and mess. Anyway de Barre wisely decided that he had no wish to make the acquaintance of Dr Guillotine's infernal machine and so, like thousands of other French aristocrats, he managed to escape and make his way to England. He and his kind were often forced to leave France with little more than the clothes they stood up in. What they lacked in financial substance they frequently made up for in arrogance and snobbishness of quite monumental proportions. This meant that they did not always make themselves welcome or popular in England as they whined peevishly about the iniquities of the Revolution in France, the vagaries of the English climate, the vapid food, the barbarity of the local population and how they couldn't wait to get back to France once sanity was restored in that country, which they thought would only be a matter of time. Many were forced to take employment which they considered debasing and menial, never having had to work before in the whole of their lives. Some got jobs as chefs and helped to bring about a transformation in the cuisine of England, or at least that part of it available to the wealthier elements of society.

Some of the French émigrés, however, did manage to thwart their pursuers by bringing large amounts of money and valuables with them to England. De Barre was one such. Even in a country they so much enjoyed loathing, some of them found Bath a relatively congenial haven and made their homes there, proceeding to establish themselves in the fashionable society of the locality. Their languid insouciance and aristocratic hauteur made them many enemies and we should not be surprised to hear that de Barre was involved in a duel on Claverton Down. There is no record of the issue over which the duel was fought, or indeed of the weapons employed, but de Barre sustained fatal injuries. The story goes that he knew he was dying and demanded a last drink. It seems unlikely that The George was the nearest watering place but nevertheless that is where he was taken. It seems that he must have expired on the premises because his ghost has reputedly haunted the place ever since. He appears from time to time, particularly in the bar, as an elusive and insubstantial shadow, normally only seen out of the corner of the eye. Apparently staff and regulars regard him as entirely harmless and even with a degree of affection.

Grey House, Batheaston

Grey House stands in this village, a short distance east of Bath. One former owner of the house was a formidable old lady whose main complaint was that she couldn't find and then retain any decent gardeners to tend the extensive grounds. This is perhaps not surprising since she spent most of her time closely scrutinising them as they worked and then telling them what a mess they were making of the task they were engaged in. She was known in those parts as 'The Lady in Purple' and this was a description of her appearance and not an affectionate nickname. In due course she went to meet her maker. Subsequently other gardeners reported that they had been busy working when they were startled to see a largish elderly woman in purple bearing down on them like a ship-of-the-line in full sail, looking wrathful and apparently about to admonish them for some shortcoming. She always vanished just before a confrontation or a fracas could have taken place.

Church of St Lawrence, Bradford-on-Avon

Bradford-on-Avon is a small town on the western border of Wiltshire a few miles south of Bath which offers a host of visual delights, not least because of its many excellent domestic buildings, particularly of the eighteenth century, and its hilliness which means that from a distance some houses almost appear to be stacked on top of others. Most are built of the mellow Bath stone and the fine detail many of them display is indicative of Bradford's former importance as a centre of the woollen industry. A walk around Bradford is a rewarding but also a strenuous experience, given the steepness of many of its streets and passageways.

Perhaps the most famous building in the town is the church of St Lawrence. The existence of a disused ecclesiastical building was only discovered in 1856 when other buildings nearby were demolished and a school and a cottage were revealed to be subdivisions of a small and simple church dating back to Saxon times. Some experts consider it to be the only complete church of the Saxon period in England. It was once known as 'The Skull House', a sinister name indeed. Could this be anything to do with the party of six tourists all of whom took photographs of the interior some years ago? They had tried to capture on film some of the interesting architectural features. What they had not bargained on was the appearance on all their developed films of a strange luminous light which had not been apparent when they had been in the building taking the pictures.

Bell, Buckland Dinham

This picturesque village is located on the A362 road a few miles north-west of Frome. The Bell is an ancient hostelry, apparently haunted by the ghost of a young girl said to have died in labour in the year 1756. The child she was bearing was illegitimate – an awful stigma at the time and she had stubbornly but bravely refused to name the father. Had she lived it would have been as a pariah. Even in death she was treated with contempt because it is believed that although the parish buried her, it was without the benefit of the full Christian ritual. It is thought that her spirit is trying to attract attention and perhaps redress for her grievances, including the lack of a proper burial. Sometimes she manifests herself by creating a sudden and unpleasant chilliness. Her figure is sometimes vaguely descried on the stairs and she seems to be able to move things about without herself being visible. On one occasion two men were dining at a table which had a candle as its centrepiece. They were startled out of their skins when the lighted candle suddenly and totally without warning jumped out of its holder and landed in the half-full pint glass of beer in front of one of the men. The Bell may date back to the sixteenth century but it is absolutely up-to-date with the service it offers. The food is excellent, it is the base for many activities in the village community and it has its own highly-regarded website!

The parish church dedicated to St Michael has one of the most attractive of the Somerset towers and a variety of gargoyles grotesque enough in some cases to give the observer nightmares. Although the word 'gargoyle' is often used to describe any odd stone carved face or other figure on the exterior of a church, strictly speaking, gargoyles project outwards from the base of the roof and have the function of throwing rainwater clear to land some distance from the base of the wall and therefore less likely to damage the foundations. The opportunity was indeed often taken to carve a comical, curious, or sometimes frightening design at the end of the projection out of which the spout protruded. The stonemasons who fashioned these items seem to have enjoyed the licence to give full rein to their imagination and sometimes the results are literally diabolical. Some students of medieval church architecture argue that the fiendish and hideous carved gargoyles were intended to have the additional function of frightening away the demons and other untold terrors which our ancestors believed lurked everywhere, especially at night.

Cannard's Grave Inn

South of Shepton Mallet, this pub stands at the intersection of five roads and had a rather gruesome signboard showing a corpse hanging from a gibbet. A former landlord of the pub was a man of criminal tendencies who was said to have enriched himself enormously by acting as a receiver of goods stolen by highwaymen and smugglers. Getting greedy, he decided to branch out into forgery but his misdemeanours were quickly detected. He knew the authorities were on his trail and rather than submit to them, he committed suicide and was buried at the nearby crossroads. Users of the pub and others travelling roads in the vicinity after dark claim that they have been scared out of their wits by a figure they catch in their headlights. He has been described as behaving manically and clutching at a sawn off rope around his neck. The result of too much scrumpy?

Dyrham

Dyrham is a hamlet in the hilly downland country north of Bath towards the M4. A young woman was an enthusiastic rider back in the 1980s and 1990s. She and a friend were enjoying a gallop on a rather overcast and humid evening when to their amazement they came across a penfold full of yellow sheep! They burst out laughing at the absurd spectacle but realised that of course the animals must just have been dipped. She caught sight of two men leaning on a nearby stone wall who also seemed amused. Sharing laughter can bring strangers together and she was prepared to shout some greeting when the men simply vanished! Without further ado the young woman took her horse and quartered the entire area looking for the men. She found nothing and, beginning to question her sanity, returned to her friend, telling her how puzzled she was. She was even more perplexed when her friend told her that she herself had seen nothing on this occasion but asked whether the men were dressed in clothes that looked about sixty years out of date. This was a fair description. How could she have known? Her friend said that she had seen the men before and knew all about their habit of suddenly disappearing. She admitted that when she rode by herself she was in the habit of smoking a joint beforehand and had seen the men several times. They had likewise vanished when she made any attempt to approach them and she had put the experience down to mild hallucination.

There is a theory that the stone walls of an area can hold images created by severe emotional events that have occurred there in the past. Under certain weather conditions, particularly those that are hot and stormy, these images can be released. Far-fetched maybe but who were the mystery men on the downs that late summer afternoon?

Farmborough

To the south-west of Bath, Farmborough is a small settlement off the A39. Its most notable building is probably the Manor House. This seems to date from the 1660s and attracts the interest of aficionados of the domestic architecture of the homes of those of middling rank at this time.

Research has not unearthed any record of there ever having been a monastery in the district so it is strange that there have supposedly been sightings of phantom nuns and even a headless funeral party. A lane in the vicinity is haunted by the ghost of a young girl who committed suicide centuries ago.

Tucker's Grave, Faulkland

Faukland is little more than a hamlet on the A366 from Trowbridge, a few miles south of Bath and not far from Radstock. The pub rejoices in the unique name Tucker's Grave. The eponymous Tucker was a local man who is said to have hanged himself in a barn close to the present inn in 1747. As was customary with suicides, Tucker was buried supposedly with a stake through his heart on unconsecrated ground thought to be where the pub's car park is now located. Although the use of the stake in this way was intended to prevent the ghost of the suicide rising from the grave and walking, it does not seem to have worked in the case of Tucker because it is said that he regularly emerges from the bowels of the earth and takes a look round, most particularly on moonlit nights. It would seem that he does not consider parked cars as any kind of obstacle to his resurrection.

Holcombe

Tucked away on unclassified roads near the A367 south of Radstock, this village has a long and hilly main street. There is a rather nondescript parish church of 1884 which replaced the previous church of St Andrew which can be found about a mile north of the village. This church, which is little used, stands remotely in a field. It has a fine reset Norman south doorway and a delightful set of wooden box-pews. Forgotten and gently mouldering rustic old churches such as this, away from human habitation, evoke a sense of poignancy even on bright, sunny spring and summer days. How much more do the spirits that inhabit such places imbue them with an eerie and ghostly atmosphere on, say, a gloomy and misty late November afternoon as dusk falls? Strong sensations would also be evoked in the very different conditions of an icy-cold and clear moonlit winter's night. In both cases it would become easy to believe that the church and churchyard contain those walking who should be resting. Few of us would venture into such places at such times for fear of 'the icy finger tracing out the spine'.

Longleat House

This well-known mansion with its lion-infested park is not far from Frome, roughly twenty miles south of Bath. The present house, completed around 1580, stands on the site of an Augustinian priory acquired by Sir John Thynne after the dissolution of the monasteries in the late 1530s. It is still in the hands of the same family. Many legends surround Longleat and give it a proud place in the list of English stately homes that are reputed to be haunted.

An enduring legend of Longleat is that an individual tragedy or even the extinction of the Thynne family will follow the departure from the lake of its fine collection of swans. In 1916 the heir to the estate was a young subaltern in the army who, like so many more of his kind, was killed in action in France. His mother claimed to have 'seen' the death of her son the day before it actually happened. On the same day she had been gazing across the lake when one of the swans took to its wings and headed off purposefully into the great blue yonder – a swan on a mission.

Several decades ago, a gardener unearthed a human skull, perhaps a relic from the priory's burial ground. A small knot of people gathered, fascinated by the discovery and a young member of the Thynne family thought that just for a lark, he would take a bike ride accompanied by the skull. Hours later he was nursing injuries resulting from a nasty fall. Four other people who had crowded round when the skull was discovered also received injuries.

Longleat's best-known ghost is the 'Green Lady'. Louisa Carteret was a beautiful young eighteenth century woman who married Thomas Thynne, second Viscount Weymouth. It was an unhappy marriage and the story is that, seeking consolation, Louisa took a lover. Thynne found out, murdered Louisa's paramour and punished her by leaving her to rue the affair.

Louisa died in childbirth aged just twenty-two and her ghost seems never to have left the house. It is an unhappy ghost and those who have sensed its presence say that it manages to cast a pall of gloom around itself and its surroundings. She is most likely to be seen in the upper parts of the house. During the installation of central heating, the remains of a young man were found under ancient flagstones.

Lord Nelson, Marshfield

Marshfield is a predominantly stone-built settlement of village size, but along its attractive main street it gives the appearance of a small town with many buildings of considerable architectural merit. The village is about six miles north-east of Bath. Happily it is now bypassed by the A420. The great west tower of the parish church catches the eye for miles around.

Why is it that so many pubs seem to have been the centre of poltergeist activity? That is a rhetorical question. To anybody who fancies they have an explanation, answers on a postcard to the publishers, please. In 1988 there were reports from the Lord Nelson of a mysterious force active mostly in the pub's kitchens. Loaves were reported as randomly flying off shelves and knives, forks and other items of cutlery mysteriously flew across the room. Items disappeared totally and were written off as lost, only to be found later, restored to their original places. Refrigerator doors were surreptitiously opened and were left that way to the detriment of the often highly perishable contents. This activity was therefore not only irksome but also scary and expensive. The behaviour of the pub dogs made it clear that they were very aware of a presence which the family and staff of the pub simply could not discern.

This case generated considerable interest locally and among the fraternity who enthusiastically investigate psychic phenomena. It emerged that the building which housed the pub had a history of sporadic outbreaks of similar activity on a number of occasions over the years. This particular burst of activity occurred during and after an extensive refurbishment. Radical structural changes in a building seem to infuriate ghosts. Perhaps they resent this intrusion into their comfort zone. They often seem to be spurred on to make their presence felt in a variety of ways even after decades or more of quiescence.

Kings Arms, Monkton Farleigh

This is a small, somewhat scattered but attractive village a few miles east of Bath with a steep main street. The pub, an ancient building, has produced reports of ghostly manifestations for many years. While many pubs have witnessed strange or inexplicable phenomena, the supernatural occurrences at the *King's Arms* are a trifle out of the ordinary. It is not often that a ghostly bird flies around the bar but this pub has just such a one. The unmistakeable sound of a large bird can be heard but the creature is never seen! Apparently the temperature drops suddenly when the sound of the bird's flight is heard. The noise is clear enough for the progress of the bird across the room to be followed. Coming to a wall provides the phantom bird with no problems – it simply flies through the wall and can be heard disappearing into the distance. Another oddity is the sound of old-fashioned navvy's hob-nail boots which are heard

Kings Arms, Monkton Farleigh

apparently ascending a flight of stone stairs despite the fact that there are no such stairs in the pub, although there may well have been some in the past.

Obviously over the years stories about this supposed haunting have been told and retold in the pub and there have been many customers who have pooh-poohed the idea of ghostly birds. Whatever it is that haunts the pub clearly takes great exception to such incredulity and it usually follows such statements by making its presence known by smashing crockery, turning on taps and leaving them running and other irritating sabotage.

Close by is Monkton Farleigh Manor. This house stands on the site of a minor Cluniac priory founded in 1125 and it contains some fragments of ancient masonry from this foundation. As so often happens with the sites of former monasteries, there have been occasional reports of phantom monks being seen moving silently around the neighbourhood. On at least a couple of occasions people claim to have heard the gentle tones of Gregorian chanting in the air and another 'witness' told the author that he heard the sound of what he described as a 'Bacchanalian orgy'. He refused to be drawn further on the matter so whether he was in the leg-pull business, having seen the author coming or the existence of the orgy was merely wishful thinking on his part, perhaps because he had always wanted to go to one, had never been invited and consequently felt left out, will probably never be established.

On a hill west of Monkton Farleigh and just inside the Wiltshire county boundary stands Brown's Folly, known locally as 'The Pepperpot'. This is easier to spot from a distance than close-by on the densely wooded hill. As follies go, it is fairly unremarkable being a rather plain tower approximately 40ft high tapering slightly towards the top. It was built in 1840 or 1848, depending on the account, by the rather eccentric Colonel Wade Brown who owned much land in the area and at least one stone quarry. Previously there had been a semaphore station at this point but it was disused and its foundations adapted for the erection of this tower. Not the least of Colonel Brown's quirks was that he was philanthropically-inclined. The area was affected by an agricultural depression which was causing considerable distress among local labourers and their families so the good Colonel decided that he could relieve some of the unemployment by employing these labourers to build a tower. Another of Wade Brown's well-meaning initiatives was to establish a village school close by and to teach in it himself although he insisted on only teaching the girls. By all accounts Wade Brown was an affable fellow well-liked by those who had dealings with him. The only possible haunting associated with the man and his tower occurred in the 1960s at dusk one evening when a lone walker claimed to have encountered a man dressed in smart Victorian clothes near the tower. He hurried past but as he did so remarked that 'they', presumably meaning the authorities, were intending to knock his tower down and as far as he was concerned they would only do it over his dead body. The walker stopped and turned round but the figure had vanished in a split second. This left the man wondering whether he had been seeing things. Perhaps Colonel Wade Brown had the last laugh. The tower had become rather ramshackle and did indeed face the possibility of ruin or demolition but it was bought by the Folly Foundation and restored to ensure its continued survival. The area surrounding the folly is now a nature reserve open to the public.

Monkton Farleigh Mine

Around 100ft under the hill on which Brown's Folly stands, lies what was for decades one of Britain's best-kept secrets. Those who knew of its existence were required by the Official Secrets Act not to reveal this information to anyone. It was virtually an underground city. It covered eighty acres and was possibly the largest underground ammunition dump in the world!

This mysterious place was located in the long defunct Monkton Farleigh stone mine. The labyrinth of caves under the hill was identified by the Government in the 1930s as having the potential for use in wartime as a storage point for ammunition and/or other war supplies. A decision was made to utilise the existing warren of caves and to create large extensions to the complex which would allow the storage of huge quantities of material deep below ground where the temperature and humidity would be more-or-less constant. After close examination it was decided that the place provided ideal conditions for an ammunition dump. A great advantage was that the erstwhile mine stood close to the main line from Swindon to Bath and Bristol owned by the then Great Western Railway and so the necessarily heavy, awkward and possibly volatile materials could be transported in and out by rail if exchange sidings were built connecting with a narrow gauge system penetrating into the hillside.

A hugely expensive building project was put into effect, costing billions of pounds by today's standards. The place had its own medical centre and power station. It is estimated that 7,500 men were employed on the construction works but only small numbers of men at any one time so that none of them were able to gain an overall idea of what the entire project involved. Security and secrecy were maintained at the highest possible level while the work was going on and even more so once hostilities had broken out. A large workforce was in place during the war consisting mostly of forces personnel but also considerable numbers of civilians and again security requirements saw to it that no one employed on the site had access to every part of the installation. Patrols and pillboxes made it inadvisable for strangers, innocent or otherwise, to get too close.

Every effort was made to try to ensure the maximum possible safety of the site. All sorts of rumours circulated in the Bath and Box areas about what exactly was going on at Monkton Farleigh and inevitably once the war started it became widely but unofficially known that explosives were stored there. The locals might have had reason to protest had they known that at the peak there were over 12 million shells stored there. A major explosion would have taken Box, Bathford and much of Bath itself with it. This is not merely idle speculation. At Fauld near Hanbury in the east of Staffordshire, the RAF had requisitioned disused gypsum mines to store bombs and ammunition during the Second World War. On 27 November 1944 for reasons unknown, there was a massive underground explosion involving 4,000 tons of high-explosive. Incredibly this was the largest detonation during the war in the whole of Europe. A crater 800ft long, 300ft wide and 120ft deep was created. At first officialdom denied that this explosion had occurred despite the loss of dozens of lives, some of the bodies remaining unaccounted for.

In the late 1970s a museum was created in the then by long disused underground complex but somehow it did not seem to catch on and it closed within a few years. All is peaceful in the Monkton Farleigh area now but traces of the former activities can be found by the determined rambler around OS grid reference 800675. No ghosts have been reported associated with Monkton Farleigh Mine but there is something undeniably eerie about this one-time hive of clandestine and sinister activity and of any remaining relics associated with it.

Fleur-de-Lys, Norton St Philip

Norton St Philip, a village a few miles south of Bath, is probably noted most for the splendid and venerable George Inn. This building has been dispensing hospitality for six hundred years and is said to have been built to accommodate merchants trading in wool and cloth with the monks of nearby Hinton Priory. It has a host of fascinating fittings, furnishings, and nooks and crannies, and looks as if it ought to have more than its fair share of ghosts as well as housing a host of memories.

Strangely enough, however, the reports of ghosts came from another pub in the village, the Fleur-de-Lys which was opposite. In 1685 the 'Pitchfork Rebellion' took place when there was an ineffectual uprising in the West Country in support of the vacuous Duke of Monmouth. Legend has it that a party of captured rebels were brought to the George, tried, found guilty and then sentenced to death, the executions being carried out in a field behind the Fleur-de-Lys. As a column of woebegone condemned prisoners shuffled miserably through a nearby gate, a local man and bystander, eager to extend to them a last minute bit of old-fashioned courtesy, held the gate open for them. This proved to be a courteous but unwise gesture because he was mistaken for one of the prisoners and seized by the guards who ignored his protestations of innocence – after all the condemned men were probably doing the same – and minutes later the poor fellow was launched into eternity.

Some claim that his ghost haunts the Fleur-de-Lys – perhaps he was a regular. He is said to be chuntering away to himself as well he might about the injustice of his fate. His presence is held responsible for the disembodied sound of jangling, said to resemble the rattling of shackles,

Fleur-de-Lys, Norton St Philip

fleeting glimpses of a shadowy figure, occasional feelings of intense cold and the undeniable but unaccountable terror shown by the pub's dogs.

Peasedown St John

This is an unexceptional settlement a few miles south-west of Bath towards Radstock and now bypassed by the A367. In 1988 and 1989 there seems to have been a brief outbreak of poltergeist activity. Unusually, this was reported as occurring in several houses around the same time. Also unusual, but probably of no significance, the locations were all council houses. While the outbreak of this activity must have been disturbing and disruptive for the occupants, it was run-of-the-mill poltergeist stuff with pictures flying off the wall for no apparent reason, small objects flying across rooms and objects irritatingly disappearing from their usual positions only to turn up elsewhere, sometimes after having apparently been lost forever, in places which had already been searched.

The poltergeist activity spread to the Waggon and Horses pub. A member of the licensee's family complained of constantly being woken up at night by an unseen hand that stroked her face, empty beer crates were thrown around the beer cellar and an unseen hand altered the pressure used in the cellar to allow the beer to reach the bar upstairs. Was the beer flat that night?

Shepton Mallet

This is a small town south-west of Bath possessing a church with an exceptionally fine wooden panelled roof, a market cross of around 1500, an ancient shambles, some old almshouses and a host of other ancient and interesting buildings.

Perhaps a fully working prison is an unexpected building to find in a place like Shepton Mallet. HMP Shepton Mallet may be small but it is nevertheless the country's oldest prison.

Shepton Mallet Prison

It opened for business in 1610. Seven judicial executions took place within its portals between 1889 and 1926, and those concerned were buried, as is the practice, in unmarked graves within the precincts of the prison. It closed as a prison but was used for storing valuable old documents until the Second World War. It was then taken over by the American forces and used as a prison once more. They were seemingly more generous in handing out executions and no fewer than eighteen servicemen died there, sixteen hanged and two shot by firing squad. After the war, it became a British military prison until 1966 when it returned to use as a civil jail once more.

The very least to be expected is that the ghost would reflect these emotive events but in fact the presence is thought to belong to a female prisoner who was executed within the prison walls in 1680 and is known as the 'White Lady'. It can be heard breathing heavily, its threatening presence is felt rather than seen and, like most of its kind, when it is close by, the temperature falls suddenly and sharply. For reasons that only it knows, it had been quiescent for years but then suddenly burst into a flurry of activity in the late 1960s with sufficient force thoroughly to scare prison officers who were on duty, especially at night-time. Since then the 'White Lady' has either been slumbering or has moved off elsewhere.

A local legend tells of an old woman called Nancy Camel who knitted stockings for a living and shocked local opinion by working on Sundays. She agreed to sell her soul to the Devil in return for a king's ransom in riches. She kept working at her trade, wisely not telling her neighbours about her wealth and the dubious way in which she had acquired it. Eventually she realised that death was approaching and she had a visit from the Devil informing her that he would soon be claiming her soul. Now she regretted the pact she had made and confessed what she had done to a priest who told her that she must throw away all the money the Devil had given her. She agreed to do this but kept back just one coin. The Devil was outraged and came for Nancy in the night during a great storm. He placed her in his cart, carried her off and she was never seen again. A cave nearby is called Nancy Camel's Hole and marks at the entrance are said to have been made by the cloven hooves of the Devil while curious grooves in the rock are alleged to be ruts left by the wheels of his cart as he seized the petrified Nancy.

Wellow

Wellow lies a few miles south of Bath. It stands in hilly and attractive country and benefits from being away from major classified roads. The fine church, rather unusually dedicated to St Julian – the patron saint of fishermen, has fabric dating back to the fourteenth century. The figure of a grey lady has been seen around the churchyard and the older buildings in the village. A well nearby is dedicated to St Julian and it is said to be haunted by the ghost of a white lady who appears, some say, just before the death of a Lord of Hungerford.

Westwood Manor

Westwood is a village not far from Bradford-on-Avon with many attractive stone-built houses. The church of St Mary has an impressive but rather curious-looking west tower, not unlike a scaled-down version of the central tower of Wells Cathedral, and very fine fifteenth-century stained glass in the east window. The manor stands close to the church. It was started about

1400 and contains work from many subsequent periods. It is open to the public.

There are two ghosts. The first is female and restricts its activities to one specific bedroom. It is more often sensed than been seen but it appears to take a perverse delight in ensuring that anyone who sleeps in the room has a thoroughly disturbed night, including even those who previously knew nothing about the bedroom's reputation. It obviously has an atmosphere because on one occasion a guest who had no knowledge of the haunting and didn't believe in ghosts anyway, refused to sleep in the room after simply opening the door and looking around. This was on the grounds that there was a feeling in the room that she couldn't define but she immediately sensed that she didn't like.

The second ghost can be seen and is menacing because in all the best traditions of the spirit world, it is headless. That is not to say that it tucks its head under its arm or anything so melodramatic but understandably it upsets people when it takes to wandering around the house. It normally does this noiselessly but it is thought to be responsible for the occasional sound of footsteps apparently pounding up, never down, one particular staircase.

Other titles published by The History Press

Bath
PAUL DE'ATH

This fascinating collection of over 200 old photographs of Bath and its surrounding villages evok
memories of a bygone age. Bath's splendid heritage of streets and buildings can be seen in anoth
age, but surprisingly much that is portrayed here will be recognisable to visitors and residents alil
Although the book contains a record of the city there is also a good selection of images from Ba
environs, its approach roads and its waterways. Paul De'Ath has compiled this book from his owr
extensive collection of historic postcards and early photographic prints.

978 0 7524 0127 0

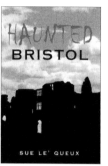

Haunted Bristol
SUE LE' QUEUX

From paranormal manifestations at the Bristol Old Vic to the ghostly activity of a grey monk wh
is said to haunt Bristol's twelfth-century cathedral, this spine-tingling collection of supernatural
tales is sure to appeal to anyone interested in Bristol's haunted heritage. This enthralling selection
newspaper reports and first-hand accounts recalls strange and spooky happenings in the city's anc
streets, churches, theatres and public houses. Here is a unique glimpse into the ghostly legacy of
Bristol's past that is sure to appeal to anyone interested in a spot of ghost hunting.

978 0 7524 3300 4

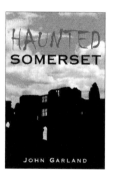

Haunted Somerset
JOHN GARLAND

This collection of stories and twice-told tales from around Somerset lifts the shrouds off many
new and legendary hauntings. Researching historical and contemporary sources, *Haunted Somerset*
reveals its uniquely supernatural heritage from a coffin on the road, eerie Bath, the phantoms of
Sedgemoor, Dunster Castle's ghostly sightings, headless horsemen, animal apparitions and Exmoor
spectres ... and if these are not enough to curdle your nervous system, a screaming skull and the
grisly haunting associated with a curate murdered by some of his parishioners – and rumoured to
have been cannibalised- certainly will!

978 0 7524 4335 5

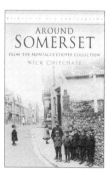

Around Somerset
NICK CHIPCHASE

Montague Cooper was probably Somerset's first commercial photographer – certainly the county's
finest. He had studios in Taunton, Burnham and Chard, and traveled widely around Somerset in or
of the county's first motor cars - often to be spotted in the background of his photographs. Nick
Chipchase has researched his life and work, and presents here a fascinating album of his work - a
true reminder of bygone days which will appeal to anyone interested in the history of Somerset.

978 0 7509 4677 3

Visit our website and discover thousands of other History Press books.
www.thehistorypress.co.uk